# CHOSEN JEWEL

## CAPRICE L. LYONS

# CHOSEN JEWEL

Copyright ©2018 by Caprice L. Lyons

All rights reserved. No part of this book may be reproduced, copied, stored or transmitted in any form or by any means – graphic, electronic, or mechanical, including photocopying, recording, or information storage and retrieval systems without the prior written permission of Caprice L. Lyons or HOV Publishing except where permitted by law.

Unless otherwise indicated, all Scriptures quotations are taken from The Holy Bible, The New International Version (NIV) Copyright 1973, 1978, 1984, 2011 by Biblica, Inc.
The NIV Study Bible (NIV) Copyright 1985, 1995, 2002, 2008, 2011
Published by Zondervan
3900 Sparks Dr., SE
Grand Rapids, Michigan 49546
www.zondervan.com. All rights reserved.

HOV Publishing a division of HOV, LLC.
www.hovpub.com
hopeofvision@gmail.com

Cover Design: HOV Design Solutions
Editor: Dianna Knox-Cooper
Editor/Proofreader: Amy A. Owens

Visit the Author Caprice L. Lyons at:
www.capricelyons.com

For more information about special discounts for bulk purchases, please visit www.hovpub.com

ISBN 978-1-942871-44-6
Library of Congress Control Number: 2018964513

10  9  8  7  6  5  4  3  2  1

Printed in the United States of America

# DEDICATION

I dedicate this book to my loving grandmother, Jewel Mae Williams. She is the reason I was inspired to write this book. My grandmother was the first "Jewel" I knew, and she is a vital part of my walk with God. She taught me so many great values through both spoken and unspoken words, and she taught me the value of jewels. Additionally, my grandmother taught me that I am special, and she cultivated the jewels that were placed in me by God and buried within me for this day and this purpose. I carry my grandmother, my *Precious Jewel*, with me every day.

# ACKNOWLEDGEMENTS

To my late father, Roy David Lyons Sr., who was not only my father, but my friend whom I adored. I got my personality from my dad; he was funny, and he loved to laugh.

To my mother, Susie Mae Lyons, who has always been in my life as my supporter and encourager to remind me that I can do anything.

To my son, DeMarquis Lyons, the greatest gift of joy that God has given me. My son is such a thoughtful young man and he has made me proud. When life gets tough he always encourages me that I can do it.

To my brother, Roy David Lyons Jr., who spoke into my life and who is an awesome big brother, my sister-in-law Cherise Lyons, my nephew Caleb A. Lyons and my nieces Shanell H. Smaw and Camryn J. Jefferies, my godchildren Brittany C. Poteat and Amauri C. Poteat, and last, but certainly not least, my best friend Tarsha R. Palmer.

To Prophetess Cynthia Carter who has been my mentor. Prophetess Carter always takes the time to pray with me and encourage me to hold on to what God has told me.

To Pastor Andy Thompson and First Lady LaShawn Thompson, my pastors and leaders who have guided me and instructed me in The Word. My life would not be the same without the careful and loving care that they give to me.

# TABLE OF CONTENTS

**PREFACE** ...................................................... 1
CHOSEN JEWEL

**CHAPTER 1** ................................................. 7
THE JEWEL OF LOVE - *Ruby*

**CHAPTER 2** ............................................... 19
THE JEWEL OF FAITH - *Emerald*

**CHAPTER 3** ............................................... 31
THE JEWEL OF CLARITY - *Topaz*

**CHAPTER 4** ............................................... 39
THE JEWEL OF FLASHING - *Carbuncle*

**CHAPTER 5** ............................................... 45
THE JEWEL OF ASPIRING - *Sapphire*

## CHAPTER 6 ................................................ 55

THE JEWEL OF ENERGY & GROWTH - *Quartz*

## CHAPTER 7 ................................................ 63

THE JEWEL OF WISDOM - *Jacinth*

## CHAPTER 8 ................................................ 71

THE JEWEL OF BALANCE - *Agate*

## CHAPTER 9 ................................................ 79

THE JEWEL OF HEALING - *Amethyst*

## CHAPTER 10 .............................................. 87

THE JEWEL OF TRUTH - *Chrysotile*

## CHAPTER 11 .............................................. 95

THE JEWEL OF POWER - *Onyx*

## CHAPTER 12 ............................................ 107

THE JEWEL OF POSSIBILITIES - *Opal*

ABOUT THE AUTHOR........................ 116

ADDITIONAL INFORMATION

# CHOSEN JEWEL

# PREFACE
## *Chosen Jewel*

---

Every woman should understand and know her worth and be comfortable in who she was created to be. It does not matter where you were when you started this life of womanhood. Instead, it matters that you undertake the process of becoming the greatest woman that you can be. This concept of knowing who you are is not only for you, but also for other women with whom you interact, or that woman who watches you from afar. As women, we are powerful and very influential. We should be quick to assist our sisters who are starting on this wonderful journey of life and also those women who have found themselves stuck because of a bad choice, or because something bad has happened in their lives. Perhaps, they just connected with the wrong people.

**What is a Jewel?**

Jewel: a precious stone; an ornament of precious metal often set with stones or decorated with enamel and worn as an accessory of dress; one that is highly esteemed; a bearing for a pivot (as in a watch) made of crystal, glass, or a gem.[1]

https://www.gemselect.com/gem

**How are Jewels made?**

There are many types of jewels and each has significant attributes. Similarly, there are many factors that contribute to what God desires for us so that we can become the Chosen Jewel that He created us to be. Jewels created by God are placed in us in Heaven. The formation of jewels in the earth are underground and they go through pressure, time, and the atmosphere. When the jewels are dug up, they are various sizes and shapes, and they have different values. Our Jewels were created in a similar way—they are formed in our spirit through pressure, time, and the atmosphere. After God's appointed time, our Jewels come forth with power, wisdom, and knowledge of the things God has given us. Yet, there are other kinds of jewels, which are man-made, these jewels are made by manufacturing. Counterfeit jewels are sent by the enemy to bring darkness and confusion, and to steal our peace. When jewels are created in a manufactory, they are made to look like the real jewel, when the enemy gives us jewels, they look real, but they are not. This is how the enemy will send confusion. These are counterfeits and without a good understanding of jewels and their value, a person can be deceived into thinking that they are the real-thing.

Whether the jewels that we own are made through natural processes (created by God), or in a lab (created by man and sent by the enemy) all of them have value. Jewels

---

[1] https://www.merriam-webster.com/dictionary/jewel

are created and produced under numerous circumstances. Within your lifetime, you may have encountered things that have given your Jewels value. Over time, the value of Jewels increases if they are kept properly. God placed Jewels within you that may have to be forged under the pressure of adversity, challenge, and perseverance. However, there are also Jewels that you have obtained from the enemy. He came to steal, destroy, confuse, and kill you. But, because you are under God's covering, the things that were forged against you are now priceless jewels. You can use those jewels to your advantage to help you grow, mature, and sustain your position. They can also help you to build up another woman.

The jewels that we were born with are gifts that reside in our souls where they have the opportunity to mature over time. Some of those jewels are love, faith, clarity, aspiring, power, singing, teaching and motivating. We have some jewels that are produced through the lab of life. These are imitations that the enemy has presented as if they are good things, though they are not. We may have worn those jewels thinking that they were priceless, but they were just knockoffs. Some of those jewels are feelings of inferiority, unworthiness, shame, guilt, hate, jealousy, and self-pity. We all have had something that was a knockoff, such as a coat, pocketbook, a wallet, etc.

**Organizing Your Spiritual Jewels**

1. Inventory – Take inventory to know the quantity and type of jewels you have.

2. Value – Understand the value of your jewels; know the worth of your love and peace.

3. Knowledge – Know the history of your jewels and understand the people and times that are connected to your Jewel.

4. Accessibility – Know exactly where your jewels are located for quick access. For example, if you need joy, you should not be looking everywhere for days to locate it.

A jewel, regardless of its origin and unique characteristics, has value. Just as each jewel in the world is different, so is each person. As women, each attribute that makes us different makes us who we are. We should take pride in ourselves and our unique facial features, tone of voice, height, skin tone, hair texture, size, age, etc. We can be critical of ourselves and may even have a list of things that we would change if we could. When we feel this way, we should ask ourselves, "If I could change something about myself, would it be something that I could change through effort and discipline, or would it have to do with changing something about the way God made me?" As we read in I Peter 2:9, *"But you are a chosen people, a royal priesthood, a holy nation, God's special possession, that you may declare the praises of him who called you out of darkness into his wonderful light."*

Salvation is not the absence of sin. It's the presence of the process, procedures, and practices to maximize your growth in knowledge and wisdom. The enemy has set out to take the value of the jewels that God placed within you and when something loses value, it's worth diminishes; ultimately it becomes worthless.

Now it is time to increase your value because you are a woman that was sent from Heaven and your value is expected to increase daily. Heaven's rules are different from earth's rules. If you look in the Kelly Blue Book or get a car appraised, they ask different questions and look for things to assess the value. Do you know what your value was when you were on Heaven's Show Room floor? You were PRICELESS! There is not a dollar amount that can equal to the value of you. So, you should not sell yourself short.

Three objectives to keep in mind while reading each chapter are:

- Look at the risks of not having the Jewels or maintaining them and understanding the benefit of Jewels.

- Utilize all your defenses and know the offenses in the protection and the upkeep of your Jewels.

- Believe that some set-backs, mistakes, and bad choices can be prevented. You do not have to experience something to learn from it. Take the advice of someone, read a book, observe others, or seek God's spiritual impartation.

# CHAPTER 1
*Jewel of Love*

## Ruby

    Ruby is an aphrodisiac, allowing one to experience all forms of love, from wild sensuality to mystical communion. It deepens a couple's relationship, bonds friends together, strengthens families and encourages closeness and commitment. It is also the stone of courtly love and may garner admiration from a distance. Worn during lovemaking, Ruby can help restore and maintain passion, and is excellent for increasing the chances for conception.

    Love is a force of nature. As much as we want it, real love cannot be bought. You can choose to surrender to love, or not, but in the end, love strikes like lightening by being unpredictable and irrefutable. It has its own chemistry, is a passionate commitment, and drives all great stories.

The Lord our God is the first one to share this precious gift of love. The love that God shares is the purest form of love. So, many things are represented in the earth by love, but nothing can compare to the example that God has given us. Quite often, when we think about love, we think of loving others in a caring way and in some cases, in an intimate way.

Loving yourself is an important part of being able to love others, as well as being able to love intimately. Learning to love yourself sounds odd, but there are some people who do not love themselves or even know how. The lack of love in the world is a major, yet silent problem, because the enemy wants to cast blame on people and have them at odds with each other. The lack of love is the cause of many issues such as conflicts, disagreements, discord, hatred, envy and strife.

When we truly love yourself, we love who we are and accept the wrong that we have done. This is not to approve of the wrong that we did, or to say that it was right because wrong is wrong and it will always be wrong. It is very important that we know the difference between right and wrong and that we are willing to acknowledge the things that we did so that we can move forward in our life, and into a healthy and honest place with our self.

It's bad to have dishonest people in our lives. At least we have the option of walking away from them, but where can we leave our self? Where we go, we follow. I will use myself as the example because I have walked on this path and I was determined, "Oh No! This will not be my life!"

Sometimes things must happen in order to get where we need to be. If you are on a path that is not going in the right direction the turning point may not be a simple and convenient solution, there may be a crash-and-burn situation. Unfortunately, I was a tough, hard headed and 'all in' type of chick. Now, I am still that chick. I kept my tenacity to be a tough, ride-or-die chick, but I have changed who I am riding for.

If you commit a crime, the courts give you a sentence based on the offense. On the first offense, you may be sentenced to just probation and fines. But on the second offense, you are usually sentenced to jail time and fines. You must do as the courts have instructed and move forward. Yes, it will become public record. This information is always available for anyone to see and some people may have the intentions to get the information to only hurt you. This is a part of life that can be embarrassing if you let it and you do not get delivered. The process of deliverance is acknowledging your wrongs, forgiving yourself and rectifying anything that you can if it is possible.

A key point to understand is that every criminal doesn't or didn't get caught.' You then must make the choice between continuing to try to perfect your criminal life and keep trying to see if you can succeed at it or change your life. It is your job to prove that you are not that person anymore by not continuing with that same behavior of wrong-doing. You will have to put the work in daily to change old habits and thoughts, it will not be easy, but it will be worth it.

# JEWEL OF LOVE

My crime was selling crack cocaine; it was my first and last charge. Can you say, "WAKE UP CALL?" I considered myself a tough cookie, but the moment I was charged, I didn't feel so tough. Things, for me, had become serious. I received 2 years of probation and fines for the sale and distribution of crack and a misdemeanor charge for marijuana.

The marijuana was for my personal use. I actually started off selling marijuana until I became my best customer and the money wasn't so great. The sale of crack was very profitable, so I chose to do that. Here is where my choices came in and I asked myself if I wanted to continue on that path or did I want to change.

The thing that I noticed about the drug-life was that so many people cannot get off the ride and they continue to go through the same cycle. The thing about the devil is that he exploits your weaknesses. Some people who sell drugs do it because they see it as glamorous. Others do it to provide for their families. They start with doing one deal and it just goes on and on. Why? Because the devil makes things look good and the shine of it blocks the view of the consequences. The devil puts stumbling blocks in your way so that you feel that there is no other way out. Very often the turning points come but it may not be enough to stop the cycle.

Can you see the old me versus the new me? They are two different people; the new me would never make that choice because of the love that I have for myself. I have been empowered by strong people who took the time to show me how to love myself. With the information that I have now, I know the cause and effect of drugs on the community and people. The drugs are part of the enemy's strategies. In John 10:10, we read that *"The thief comes only to steal and kill and destroy; I have come that they may have life and have it to the full."*

When I got caught and received my sentence, my first probation officer was a woman. I walked into her office for my first appointment. She looked at the file and looked at me. Then she looked at the file again and looked at me and asked me, "What are you doing here?" I just looked at her, remaining silent because I was confused; I did not know what she meant. I knew that I had an appointment with her about my probation, but she was not talking about my appointment, she was talking about my Jewel. The light from our Jewel will be so illuminated in the presence of others that they may see it before we even know that it is there.

The probation officer went on to say that I did not look like the others and that most of the people that come into her office looked and acted a certain way and that I did not look or act like they did. Do you know that you are being identified and categorized by people you may not even talk to? I am not sure who the probation officer expected to see for her appointment that day but whatever stereotype or preconceived idea she had I changed it.

When you deal with people long enough you just know certain things about their character without much conversation or interaction with them. First impressions are a lasting impression. Make sure that your first impression is a good one and that you carry yourself like you want to be perceived. When my good sense came in, I realized that I had to do something because I could not live my life making reckless choices and having someone else look at me and see something in me that I could not see for myself.

During and after the completion of my two-year probation, it was my responsibility to prove to the people around me who I was becoming. I could not get mad when they considered me a menace to society or a person who destroyed lives, because that is what I had done. I sold poison to people for a profit. I had to make a decision to ask God for forgiveness and I had to forgive and love myself and move on.

Do I approve of what I did? No. Do I accept what I did? Yes. Am I sorry for the people whose lives were hurt within that time? Yes. This is a part of what has made me strong and resilient. Would I go back in time and change this part in my life if I could? No, because I know today I made it through it and I know that in life everyone will make choices that will not only affect their lives, but others, and that everyone will not get the good out of every decision.

The valuable lesson that I learned from the pains of this experience is that it cost me something. There is a price to pay for living this life. I learned to appreciate life and the freedom it offers. It could have been another outcome. When you endure certain types of pains in life you will remember them, and that memory will keep you from doing the same thing again.

I love God more and more each time I think of how far He has brought me and how He has changed my life, I would not want to give up the feeling of gratitude that I have. I have taken what I have learned and applied it to my life and with that experience, I have added to my love formation.

I share this because there may be someone reading this who has made a choice similar to those I've shared, or something similar, and is wondering, "What now?" The 'what now' is LOVE. Until we love ourselves, we are good for no one. If we don't believe in love, we cannot love. If we don't believe that we can be loved, we will not be loved. If we have unhealthy stipulations about love, it will be hard for someone to love us. We have to get that fixed. Love will enable each of us to be like a magnet that is drawn to others who know how to love correctly; we can be examples to each other. When we accept that we are not alone in the struggle, we learn how to love ourselves and others. Then our healing process can begin.

The interesting thing about this story is that although I was not saved, the Jewels inside me were calling me to a better place. I had to love myself enough to trust the feeling inside me and to trust God, who I only knew casually.

The apartment that I stayed in, where I obtained all my illegal drug possessions, burned to the ground when the couple living next door got into a fight. When God started me over, I could not take all that corruptible stuff with me. He started me with a firm foundation and I got more with Him than I had selling drugs. I got saved nine months later. Even though my turn-around had to be a crash and burn, God knew what it took to get my attention. If you are at a turn-around point, or in the midst of a crash and burn, there is life after. There is a price to pay for your anointing. You will appreciate everything thing that you do and get when God begins to reteach and restore to you.

If we venture into the broken relationship where love, trust and betrayal are involved, it can be devastating. However, the good news is, you can recover. We can all attest to a broken heart from someone we loved, whether it was from a spouse, parent, friend, child, co-worker, etc. It is vital that you overcome the hurt or betrayal through love and forgiveness, no matter whose fault it was.

There is no way that we can explain pain; everyone has a different threshold for pain. Every mother who has given birth has a different story to tell. Although each achieved the same results, the baby comes through different processes and pain. I have learned to not minimize a person's pain because everyone is different. You may endure certain things in life and bounce back, but someone else may not be able to bounce back as quickly. By no means does this mean that the less strong person should stay weak and remain a victim. There is a difference from a slow come back and no come back.

A part of hurt is to know our part, where we are and what we need to do to be better and wiser. The repeating of a hard lesson is never good or fun; we should try to learn as soon as possible. Brokenness has a way of burying itself and it will hide itself deep until it exposes itself. Most of the time when we have an area that is not good, we should be aware that unhappiness, evil, and darkness tries to take over everything good or anything with promise. So, if we have any unresolved issues, just know that it will show up in our good places and unresolved issues will not fade unless we do the work to resolve them.

Let me use myself as a prime example. I stated earlier that I was a drug dealer. But, before I dealt drugs, I was a smoker of crack. That is backwards right? Most dealers become addicts because they begin to use their products. God delivered me from using drugs. However, through my brokenness, I did not allow God to fix me. When the brokenness showed up, guess who was waiting on me, the devil. This left me open to fall into something that looked good to me. One deal led to another, then another, and then I was caught up in that fast life.

Understand me, this thing is real! You cannot play with it because you can never outsmart God and you are never devious enough to play with the devil. The devil is so crafty that he will persuade you to do something when you know your answer should be, "NO." The enemy is a smooth operator he will say things to you such as, "Let me ride with you." He will get in your car and ride with you for a while. Then he will turn and look at you and say, "Move over, you are driving too slow, let me drive." And when he takes over, you will be everywhere.

The enemy's goal is for you to live life fast, giving no thought to what you are doing or the consequences of your actions. On a normal day, doing your daily routine, you sometimes forget things. You may lose your keys or phone. Imagine what would could happen if the enemy pushed and rushed you all day. How long do you think that would last before you break?

I do not say this to hype the devil up. I want you to know he is real and he means to kill you if he gets a chance. Those unresolved issues come with lots of negative emotions, feelings of unworthiness, and low self-esteem that will make us feel like that is who you are.

We will need the power of love to keep us in the right place. We have to trust God and move forward and try again, because there must be another again. Once we accept it, ask for God's forgiveness and forgive ourselves, then God can begin to heal us so that we can be normal, productive, and functioning women in the world.

I have learned to love myself by learning to accept who I was, who I am, and who I will be. By accepting all the wrong and bad things I have done, it also helps me to understand the lack of love that I had for myself back then. And today it keeps me from returning to that place.

Proverbs 26:11 says, *"As a dog returns to his own vomit, so a fool repeats his folly."* 2 Peter 2:20-22 also says, *"If they have escaped the corruption of the world by knowing our Lord and Savior Jesus Christ and are again entangled in it and are overcome, they are worse off at the end than they were at the beginning. It would have been better for them not to have known the way of righteousness, than to have known it and then to turn their backs on the sacred command that was passed on to them."*

This portion of scripture from Proverbs is true, "A dog returns to its vomit," and, "A sow that is washed returns to her wallowing in the mud." The dog is obviously sick from what he has eaten, and he vomits to get whatever he has eaten out. Later he returns and eats the vomit again because it is in his nature. The sow is clean, but it is her nature to get dirty again after she has been washed. God is trying to break that sinful nature and if it is not broken we will find ourselves back eating the vomit and wallowing in mud of sin again. Can you see yourself as a dog or a sow going back to a situation that you were free from? Love will keep us from returning to that place. Love will keep us where we need to be so that we are strong enough to avoid the temptations.

Once I embraced love for myself, I overcame the bad choices that I made. Love is powerful and calming; it can change your emotion. We don't have the time to continue to allow those things that have happened to us, whether we did it or someone did it to us, hold us in a place that is not good. Don't allow something that happened long ago to continue to define who you are. The characters in the story of our past are long gone. The script is only being rehearsed by us. Let's rewrite our story so that we win and move on.

If we don't allow ourselves to embrace love, it will vex our own soul. We will pass everyday reliving the old mistakes, choices, and decisions that we made when our knowledge was limited. Now that there are so many ways to learn and to obtain information through technology, we can learn and get the assistance that we need. It is time to "Be Free!"

As women, love is very important to us. We must know how to keep it, give it, guard it, respect it, and cherish it. It is love that makes the Jewels in us so valuable. It is because of the things that we have seen, heard, and experienced; the rights and the wrongs, the good and the bad that have made our love one of a kind and unique.

Just like jewels, no two women are the same. No woman is the same and no woman's love is the same. It is imperative that we learn to love ourselves, so that the love that was forged under the pressures of life, shine forth and can be seen and experienced by the world. The world is waiting on us. Women are creatures who are nurturers. To nurture is to support and encourage, as during the period of training or development; foster to; feed and protect; to bring up; train and educate. To nurture is to love.

"Who you were, who you are, and who you will be are three different people." (unknown)

**Jewel of Love**

Above all guard your heart (where your love is stored) for it determines the course of your life. (NLT). Maintain this Love Jewel at all costs; everything you do flows from it. The Love Jewel is the essence of who you are and it controls your ability to function. If love is not stored and nurtured correctly, it can lead to many dysfunctions.

***Declaration:***

Today I will begin to love myself totally. Today I will love the woman that I was, even though she did not know how to love herself. Today I am woman enough to love the brokenness that was within me. I forgive myself; I release any negative emotions of my past and I accept all my responsibilities. I will love who I am today because I have survived some of the toughest things in my life. I love myself for hearing truth and by walking in it. I will truly love myself enough by not returning to unhealthy thinking or living. I will treasure my Jewel of Love and share with others the powers that it has. I will share my past to help others because I am free, and I want them free. Amen

# CHAPTER 2

*Jewel of Faith*

## Emerald

The emerald has long been the symbol of hope.

Faith is defined as belief with strong conviction; firm belief in something for which there may be no tangible proof; complete trust, confidence, reliance or devotion. Faith is the opposite of doubt. Hebrew 11:1 (KJV) states, *"Now faith is the substance of things hoped for, the evidence of things not seen."*

Faith is something that we all want more of. Oftentimes, we like to skip the steps to obtain the faith muscles to activate the faith that we need to get to the places that we need to get to. Everyone has faith for certain things. We have faith to use toothpaste and believe that the brand we've chosen will brighten and clean our teeth like the description on the box told us it would. We have faith to believe that when we turn the light switch on the lights will work.

For some reason, we tend to separate the different types of faiths. There are times where we can have faith in things that do not take much effort for us to believe and then there is faith that takes effort to believe. The reason that faith is easier about the toothpaste is because we used it yesterday and it worked. You have never heard of any one's teeth falling out because they used toothpaste.

When we have to active our faith muscles and work our faith for health, marriage, children, money, or for a job, we have to put the work in and there is a possibility that there will be failure or disappointments. There may be a long time in our faith walk that we have to wait before the evidence of what we are believing for manifests itself. We can have more faith in some areas than others. Why? Because we have used that faith muscle to believe for more and we saw the results of our prayers, which made it easier. When we are believing for a new thing, that takes new faith. Legitimate faith does not solve uncertainty and does not give answers to every question. The uncertainty in faith enhances our senses to beware of timing, possibilities, and experiences.

I had to believe God for a better life and I had to believe that I deserved it. I had to believe that my life was more than selling drugs, doing drugs, drinking, smoking cigarettes and partying. See, I had a lot going on. There was never a dull moment with me and the more you read, you will know it. If He can change me, He can change you. I believed this about myself and I was not saved. The Jewels that were buried in me, were being activated by the call of God on my life. I did not understand the pull because the synthetic jewels the enemy was throwing my way, were making me into a person who was the opposite of my destiny.

We all know that famous saying, "Everything happens for a reason." This is a factor that will always be, as long as we live, "the pull." The enemy puts synthetic jewels in our life hoping to blind us so that we will see differently about ourselves and our lives. Thanks be to God that He can, and will, turn things around to work in our favor. God uses what the enemy intended to destroy us with to advance the Kingdom.

I really did not know the protocols of how to approach God, but as time passed, my relationship with God got better. Contrary to what some people may believe, talking to God gets easier the more you do it. I was so scared at first because of how God was described in the Old Testament. He took out the whole family; He did not play with people.

I had a grandmother who was a God-fearing woman and she taught me the ways of God. I watched what she did, and I imitated her because I saw the affects that it had on her life. She was the type of grandmother who got on her knees and prayed for hours.

One night I wanted something out of the refrigerator. Back in the day, you asked first. You did not go get anything without asking and getting an answer. Okay, I already stated that I watched her. I went into her bedroom and saw her praying, so I walked out and waited. Time went by, I went back into her bedroom and said, "Grandma if He don't know what you meant by now, He just don't need to know. What is taking you so long? What are y'all talking about?" My grandma never stopped praying. She was probably praying for me and I didn't know it. I did not understand the relationship that my grandmother had with God.

Can you see the type of child that I was? I just spoke my mind, words were unfiltered. I had gotten to the point that I was tired, and I was sick and tired of being sick and tired. I was going to church; it was attendance and observation, but I remembered my grandmother on her knees praying to God and He changed things for her. So, I figured why not just ask Him? I told God, "If this is life, you can come on and get me because life has to be better than this!" I was not suicidal. I knew this could not be what life was about and I knew I was not living life.

The reality is that nothing synthetic can compare to the real thing and, at some point, the variation in the two will begin to show. The question is, "Are you willing to see it, listen to it and move on the call to come out of that which is not real?"

We had revival at my home church. The preacher began to prophesy to everyone and when he got to me, he looked at me, laughed and said, "I will come back to you." He went on to prophesy to other people and then came back over to me saying, "You might as well get saved because you are not doing anything else," and he walked off. When the authentic call on your life appears and confronts you, it requires an answer. Actually, if you are not saved and filled with the Holy Ghost, you are not doing anything.

As a child, I was always asking my cousins and my friends about God. It was like every time I saw them, I had a question. I did not know that He was calling me; I just thought I was being very curious. John 6:44 states, *"No one can come to Me unless the Father who sent Me draws them, and I will raise them up at the last day."* I was so fed up I said, "God, if You are as bad as they say You are, then do it! Change me!" Okay, remember, I am talking about God and He was on it. The change happened so fast that I stopped cussing and having sex! At that point in my life, I was already delivered from selling and doing drugs. I told God, "Hold up! I can get with all the other stuff but let's go slow on the sex part! That takes time. God, You are doing too much."

He said, "No. Case closed!" At that point. I GOT SAVED! I know you may be saying that my communication with God was awful. It worked for me and it was just like that. Can you see me down at the 'The Potter's House?' He worked on me and I stayed on the wheel. Of course, I know how to reverence Him and I know how to approach Him today. If you are rough around the edges, He will help you. Don't avoid His help and guidance based on how you are or what someone else says you should be doing, your relationship with God is personal. This is a personal thing.

Life is a learning process. This is why my praise is so real today. I love the Lord with all my heart because He could have taken me out in my ignorance. I have my right mind and I don't have any disorders. If I did not tell people, they would not and could not associate my former drug life with my life now. God did not allow me to lose my ability to process and comprehend. Some people who have used drugs are barely functional.

At that time, I was so in love with this guy, that I thought I could not live without him. One night while sleeping, I had two dreams in one. In the dream it was just like I was looking at myself on a TV screen. I was watching myself in both dreams. In the first dream, I dreamed that I had a baby. I had promised myself that after I had my son that I was not going to have any more kids until I was married. In the second dream I contracted a disease that there was no cure for. I knew it was a God-given dream because I never had an experience like that. Now there is one thing that I do not mind sharing about myself and that is, I am not afraid to say, "Okay, that is too much for me."

After that night was done, I was like, "God, you do not have to tell me twice." When the guy that I was talking to came over and started making his moves on me and I said, "No!" He was like, "What's wrong with you?" He knew I was always down with the sex part. I said, "Nothing I am not having sex anymore." He asked, "Why? Is it because you have someone else?"

I said, "No I am not having sex until I get married." He was mad, of course. I knew deep down he did not believe me, and he figured because I loved him so much I would give in. He asked me how I could make a decision like that without talking to him. I told him that I did not have time to talk to him God spoke and that settled it. We must realize that when God shows up in our situations, the encounter that we have with Him will be one that changes our perspective about who we are and where we are going. We must be able to discern it so that we don't miss the opportunities. Remember, some opportunities only come once.

I had to have faith that God would change my life, but this was not an easy process for me. I went from using and selling drugs into an unhealthy relationship. I could not get out of this vicious cycle of having hard challenges. Don't allow the cycle of chaos to steal your faith and your ability to believe that you are better and you deserve it.

I wanted to hold on to him and have God too. He would still come over and spend the night. He respected my choice and he would not force himself on me; but I thought if I loved him right he would then love me right and choose to get saved too. I did not want to force him to choose me because I knew that would not be his choice but mine.

Nothing truly changes if it is not genuine. If there is no respect, cut your ties and RUN! You better run and run as fast as you can! Things will not change because love is respect. No one who loves you will allow you to sacrifice yourself while they give up nothing in return. If it is really love, there is nothing that will be able to keep you apart. The sacrifices will be made. Excuses will be a way to prolong what they really want to say such as, "You are not the one," or "I really don't want to be with you."

When he stayed overnight, he would be sleeping like a baby and I would be up crying all night because I was torn. I wanted God to change my life and I believed (I had faith) that He would. But I had to do what He said do. I wanted to have sex with my boyfriend, but I was scared. Every time he stayed, the next day I would be so tired. I could not get any sleep because the Holy Ghost was there watching and talking. It was torture. I finally had to stop him from staying over because that was pure temptation.

1 Corinthians 10:12-14 says, *"So, if you think you are standing firm, be careful that you don't fall! No temptation has overtaken you except what is common to mankind. And God is faithful; he will not let you be tempted beyond what you can bear. But when you are tempted, he will also provide a way out so that you can endure it."*

God will make a way of escape. However, Luke 4:12 says, *"Do not put the Lord your God to the test."* If God has given you instructions, do not test Him by continuing to do something that He has told you not to do. No one knows when God has had enough of your behavior. Who can save you from the Hand of God?

Whatever we do, we must not play with sin like that. Not having sex was not easy either. That takes discipline. I can remember crying all the time because I thought God was just mean. God took all my pleasures. I felt like that was not living because those things made me happy. My first two years into celibacy were the hardest. I was crying all the time and asking God for a husband and I was not even ready for a husband. I just wanted the sex to be justified.

I had been living in this house for two years, after the fire in the apartment complex where I previously lived. When I was in the apartments, where I had my drug addiction and sold drugs, my mom and son lived there. I hated the apartment because it only had two bedrooms and one bathroom. I prayed to God and said, "I need to move. I don't care if it is in a house with a basement and I have to pee in a bucket." That is how fed up I was with living in that small apartment.

Well, after the fire I moved into a house that had a basement with a full bathroom. My mom and son were upstairs, and I was downstairs. God gave me what I asked for. On the way through transition, God will honor your prayers. God will make the changes in your life to get you on the right path, this is one way that He shows His faithfulness. God said that He will never leave or forsake you.

One day my flesh rose up and I said, "This is not the life for me. I am going to go holla at this dude." When you are at home you can turn all your lights off and walk around in the dark because you are familiar with the house. On this particular day, when I was in my flesh and telling God what

I am going to do, I was walking at a good pace in the dark and walked right into the wall and hit my head. I said, "Okay, God I am going to sit down. You don't have to tell me again." Not that I did not hear Him the first time when He told me, "Stop! No sex!"

Faith will come at a price. The price depends on where we are and what the call is on each of our lives.

A couple of months later my flesh rose up again. I told myself, "I will not live like this. I am going out to find somebody!" There were some stairs that went to the main floor because I was in the basement. I went to go up the stairs and missed the whole step! I scraped my leg and blood started to run down my leg. I walked myself over to the bathroom, cleaned my wound and sat on the bed. I said." God, you have my attention."

When you have faith about something in your life, there will be a time when changes will have to be made in the things you do and in your relationships with people. It does not matter whether it is having faith for a business, a spouse, a promotion, children or a scholarship. God will require a sacrifice. God will require you to give up something; it's almost like a good faith offering. When you make a deal with someone, the other person may ask that you give them something to show that you are for real about what you said, or you may have to sign a contract to hold you to it. If you break the deal, you have to pay the consequence. It is the same way with God. You have to show Him that you are for real.

Exodus 34:14 says, *"Do not worship any other god, for the LORD, whose name is Jealous, is a jealous God."* He was my sacrifice and it hurt me to the core when I had to give him up. I felt like I was all alone. It seemed like I was being isolated and I felt that it was unfair. This was the time that God needed to get my attention because I had too many distractions.

John 4:1-30 can be summarized by saying, just like the Samaritan woman at the well, the disciples were with Jesus on His journey. But when He went to the well, the disciples were not with Him, they went to go get food. Jesus had His conversation with her in private. God does not need an audience when He deals with us.

In those critical times in our lives when we are dealing with faith, especially if we are doing something that is not familiar, and it requires faith, we have to stay focused. As women we have the gift of gab. We talk and talk. When God is giving us revelation and direction it is not the time to second guess Him and ask someone else what they think about what He said. The most important thing to remember is that we cannot worry about how people will feel when God tells us to break free from them. Yes, we want to be tactful when separating ourselves but if they don't understand, leave that part to God. If they are meant to be in our lives, they will be. If they are truly our friends and they understand our worth and where we want to be, they will know that this is preparation and this season will pass.

No matter what life has been to us, particularly if it has been unfavorable, we should choose right now to have faith and believe God for better for ourselves. Change is not easy, but it is well worth it. Staying the same is not easy either, especially if we are dealing with emotions of discomfort. We are continually asking and searching for answers because we will have to deal with those feelings in the pit of our stomach that nag at us all the time. Why be taunted? Face it. Changing, or un-changing, takes work. With change, we will have to unlearn behaviors and with unchange we continue to build negative on top of negative. Unchange will have us looking at our lives with regret about what could have been. Time is always our enemy when we waste it by not doing what it takes to move.

**Jewel of Faith**

Having Faith to believe for something is an ongoing thing. The Jewel of Faith is so important because it is the lifeline that gets us from one dream to another, and from one destination to another. Without this Jewel it is impossible to make life happen. Faith gives us a boost when things seem like they are not going to work out. Faith keeps dreams alive. Faith helps us when people we love have a problem with who we are becoming and with our progress. Faith moves mountains. Matthew 17:20 says, *"He replied, "Because you have so little faith. Truly I tell you, if you have faith as small as a mustard seed, you can say to this mountain, 'Move from here to there,' and it will move. Nothing will be impossible for you."*

***Declaration:***

Today I realize Faith is essential to me because it is a hope for me to be what God has purposed me to be. I know that my faith will be tested, and I have full confidence in You God, that I will not be moved. Faith guarantees me my destiny. God has put a standard in place called faith. That faith is for me to believe in Him and that He cares about me too. I will us my faith to pull what I need out of the supernatural into the natural. I will live by faith and not by sight.

# CHAPTER 3

*Jewel of Clarity*

*Topez*

    Topaz is a balancing and calming stone that balances emotions, releases tension, and can bring joy.

    Clarity: the quality or state of being clear; the quality of being easily understood; the quality of being easily seen or heard.

    Clarity has a powerful influence over our thought process and how we comprehend things. Have you ever gone to the beach and put your feet into the water and you were unable to see your feet because the water was brown and cloudy? Have you gone to a beach where the water was clear and blue, and you could see the bottom of the ocean and everything in there where you are standing? I can tell you, the sight of seeing clear blue water and being able to see everything in the water is better than a cloudy view. We must have a clarity in our mind to make sound decisions. We need a clear mind to be free.

1 Peter 5:8 says, *"Be alert and of sober mind. Your enemy the devil prowls around like a roaring lion looking for someone to devour."* 1 Peter 1:13 also says, *"Therefore, with minds that are alert and fully sober, set your hope on the grace to be brought to you when Jesus Christ is revealed at His coming."* James 1:8 says, *"He is a double-minded man, unstable in all his ways."* When we are faced with crossroads in life we will need a clear mind to make that decision and be able to stick with it.

This is something that I always keep in mind on my journey. I was able to hold to this principle of keeping a clear mind because of my experience with crack cocaine. When I was 18-years old, an older friend of mine introduced me to crack and I became a user. She was 32-years old and I did not know anything about crack. The only drug that I had experienced at that time was marijuana. She used the drug around me and I asked her to let me try and I began to use it. Within the timeframe of my addiction I stopped three times. The third time was through the power of Jesus and I have been 22 years clean! When I was sharing this story of my testimony the question came up if I blamed my friend for introducing me to the drug? I said, "No. It was my choice." I could not go through life blaming her or holding her for something that I chose to do. I realized when I was set free that both of us were in bondage. I visited her in New York she is clean, living a great life and serving the Lord. We praised God for what He has done in our lives. Clarity will allow us to take ownership in what we have done in our lives.

# JEWEL OF CLARITY

We cannot go through life blaming everyone for things that has happened in our lives.

Won't He do it? My experience with crack was within a 7-year span with me quitting once for 10 months and another time for about 6 months. When I was praying, again, I was not saved, and I had not accepted Jesus as my Savior. I was getting high and I said, "God I do not want to do this anymore." There is something about when a person uses any type of drugs. When they are sober they think straight, and they plan not to use and plan all the positive moves and accomplishments they are going to do. But when they start using drugs all those thoughts and plans go away. The same was for me, but this time I noticed that I had sober thoughts even when I was using.

When you are not sober, you will forget about you and what is important. In 1 Peter 5:8 it states, *"Be alert and of sober mind. Your enemy the devil prowls around like a roaring lion looking for someone to devour."* I am not sure when God heard me, but I do know that He did and He helped me. One day the taste and the desire were gone. I still had work to do. I had to not go get drugs or hang around people that did it.

Influence is powerful and entertaining the wrong people can put you back where you started or in a worse condition. The power of influence can work without a person even using the drug. They can use the influence of word persuasion. One thing about knowing the streets is you learn the hustle. That is why I did not take a chance of being around anyone who was not a good person. I had to have clarity to ask God. I had to have clarity to not make the bad choices and I had to have clarity to believe that I could do it. Like I said, clarity is very important to get to the next place in your life. If we are going through something that is taking our clarity, God will stay the hand of the enemy so that we can make a conscious decision to ask for help.

I was off drugs a little over six months and one day I went around some of my family, but I did not fit in. They talked differently and they laughed about things that I did not get the punch line to. Although I had fun being with them, I wasn't comfortable and had a feeling of insecurity and shame. The enemy loves when we allow our insecurities and shame to push us away from something good and positive. The enemy will use this to isolate us. I remembered when I was around the people that I usually would hang with; I felt normal. Even though being with them was not productive, I felt comfortable. We can't allow the familiarity of people to hold us hostage in an environment that is only destroying the person that we are meant to be.

We can't allow our negative feelings to keep us in a place because we are comfortable. Nor can we allow the feelings that make us feel uncomfortable in a positive place make us run. Feelings can be deceiving; the weather can cause your emotions to change. If it is raining outside we don't want to go to work and the rain makes us want to sleep all day. But if it's sunny outside, we are ready to ride out.

Like-minded people like to hang with each other. Alcoholics like to be with alcoholics, thieves like to be with thieves, liars like to be with liars, etc. We are most comfortable around our kind. If you are shady, the people you like to hang with are shady. If you are a good and productive person, you like to be around good and productive people. When I got by myself, I was wondering why I felt different in both situations. I made a decision to not let the uncomfortable feelings scare me away.

My cousin's wife got a couple of my cousins together, so we could hangout. We went out to a restaurant and after we ate, the waitress brought us each our own separate bill. I got my bill and was getting ready to go to the cash register to pay and she said, "No, you do not take the money to them. They will take it from you and bring you back your change." I had a look on my face that you have when you are trying to process something. When she saw my expression, she said, "I am sorry I did not mean to embarrass you."

I looked at her and said, "Girl, no. Thank you, I did not know." See I had never been to a restaurant like that. The only places that I had gone to were McDonalds, Wendy's, Hardee's, Pizza Hut, Burger King, and places like that. I am not afraid of intelligent people; I have clarity about that. I know what I know, and I know what I don't know. There are Jewels that you have inside you that you will not know that you have until life activates them. The boldness that I have is a Jewel and for me being so comfortable with myself, I learned through my process that those are my Jewels. You will have to make up in your mind to embrace clarity and be crystal clear about every aspect of who you are, and who you are not.

I could have turned on my cousin's wife and acted like she was trying to be a know-it-all and not admit that I did not know, but I accepted her help. I have a lot of respect and love for her. Among the things that I adore about who she is are her beauty, genuineness, and intelligence. She walks in her intelligence and she is not afraid to be who she is, and this allowed me to be okay with where I was in my understanding. She is a woman who has earned her stripes and I will forever respect her for her gentle and caring spirit. Not only because of what she did for me, because what she did for me, she did not even know she did it. She was walking in the knowledge and I was coming into knowledge. I will always love Tasha Allen.

People tend to throw shade on others because they know more than them but that's just showing their position of not having good clarity and being insecure about themselves. Some people may say, "Oh, it wasn't such a big thing." I would say to them, case in point; when we don't have knowledge and we have to get it, it becomes priceless. Let's not let anyone minimize our growth to become better because no one can walk our walk but us. I had to fight past the cloudy feelings that were keeping me in some unhealthy emotional places. When we want better, we have to be alert about our emotions. If I had given in to my insecure feelings, I could have easily gone back to doing drugs to feel comfortable.

We need human connections in life. We should make sure that we choose the correct connections and that we are doing the right things to have those connections. I separated myself from all the people that I hung with. When I was totally free, I did not go to a rehab center, it was the touch of God. I would not go out of the house unless it was to work or church. I did not accept any phone calls. If anyone called the house phone, I had told my mom to say that I was not there. My mom was more than happy to tell them. I knew if I allowed myself to go back, I would be worse than I was before. Like I said before, it was my third time quitting. The two times that I quit on my own, I started back again it was more intense.

Matthew 12:43-45 says, *"When an impure spirit comes out of a person, it goes through arid places seeking rest and does not find it. Then it says, 'I will return to the house I left.' When it arrives, it finds the house unoccupied, swept clean and put in order. Then it goes and takes with it seven other spirits more wicked than itself, and they go in and live there. And the final condition of that person is worse than the first. That is how it will be with this wicked generation."*

When we know our previous condition, we ought not go back for our own sake. No one can really verbally explain what they went through. I don't care how many times they tell the story. And when we retell our story the person listening is not walking those exact footsteps or experiencing the same emotions. The experience is not totally complete in its horror or pain. Why would we do it again? Why go back? No temptation should be able to tempt us.

I had gotten to a point where I could stand myself and I knew I did not want to go back there. When we want clarity, we must put ourselves first because we are important. We must think clearly about what our goals are, what our next steps will be, what short-term changes we can make, and what long-term changes we can plan for. The best way to see with clarity is through the eyes of being honest with ourselves about who we are. Sometimes we paint a picture of ourselves that is far from the truth. Yes, we want to have all the good qualities and be the best, but that's not always the case. Unless we can be honest about our flaws and the things that we need to improve on or change, our clarity is only going to be but so clear through our eyes.

It is very important as we start growing and learning that we don't revert to those diluted behaviors when others are not able to accept who we are becoming. If we are sensitive, this may be harder for us because we may be concerned about other people's feelings. We don't have to be rude, but we have to be firm in our decision. People can be the master of manipulation over people who are weaker and more sensitive than they are. Clarity is knowing the person that we are, what we like, what we don't like, what we are willing to put up with, and what we are not willing to put up with. It is setting boundaries that others will have to respect to be a part of our life. Our differences may scare people; they may not accept the new us. Not because they don't want better for us, but they may be afraid of where they will fit or they may not want to face the changes that they need to make in their lives in order to stay connected to the new us. Our changes for the better should cause our friends and loved ones to exam their lives to implement necessary changes. There may come a time when it is best to move on.

**Jewel of Clarity**

There are two options for our view of the Jewel of Clarity, our eyes and our mind. We use our mind to dream, and our eyes to see. We think clearly of what we want and where we want to be, and then we see ourselves there. Clarity will allow us to chase after the vision and the path will be clear. It's time to run for it!

*Declaration:*

I am Unique. I am Strong. No one walked my walk but me. No one really knows what it takes to be me. Being me has been, and continues to be, an adventure; but I am me. I have made a choice to be better and stronger every day. I choose Clarity to help be my guide. In order for me to do this, I must have Clarity about who I am and what my worth is. I can see. I can see the beautiful me.

# CHAPTER 4

*Jewel of Flash*

## Carbuncle

**Carbuncle:** In Isaiah 54:12, the Hebrew word is 'ekdah, used in the prophetic description of the glory and beauty of the mansions above. Next to the diamond, it is the hardest and most costly of all precious stones.

**Flash:** to shine or give off bright light suddenly or in repeated bursts; to appear quickly or suddenly; to move or pass very quickly.

Have you ever been in a situation and it was almost like a flash of light or revelation came to you? In that moment, it was like you were at the end of your rope and you didn't know what to do. It's like dying, and the revelation of what you heard resuscitated life back into the situation such as the use of a defibrillator.

When I was a child, my grandma Jewel had a little white station wagon. Now this was not the big version station wagon, this was the escort style. The car would be packed to the max. There was my grandmother, who was driving, my aunt (my grandma's daughter) my three cousins, my brother, and me in the car. There was a total of seven people in this little car. She would take us with her when she would go on her errands to town or to work in the fields. On this particular day, it was so hot outside, but my grandmother would only allow us to crack all four of the windows just a little bit. It was like how dog owners today crack the windows just enough so that the dog doesn't suffocate or get overheated when the dog is left in the car by itself.

We were all riding down the road playing and laughing like kids do. The atmosphere was loud. Because we were playing and had minimal air circulation, we started to sweat which made it very uncomfortable. I looked over at my grandmother and she was singing her gospel songs and tapping her fingers on the stirring wheel. To my surprise, there was not one drop of sweat on her face! She was alright. I said, "Grandma, can we let the windows down? It is hot in here?"

She said "No."

I asked her why and she said, "No, because it will slow the car down. When the wind gets inside the car it pushes the car back and it will cause the car to use more gas to pull it and I don't have that much gas in the car." We were so hot that we just sat still in the car, not playing and we were not talking anymore. I can only imagine that my grandmother was in the car wishing that we would shut up making all that noise and be still. Now she never once told us to be still or shut up. She let us figure out what we needed to do to make ourselves comfortable. She used what she had to get us to be quiet. I did not get the revelation to this story until I was much older. I would drive my car with the windows cracked when I did not have much gas in the car because I thought I would save gas.

    I was going through a financial situation in my life where I had saved my money for a down payment on a house and then it was all gone. I lost my money. I was not able to get my house. I had just lost my $2,000 down payment for the house and I was so mad! I did everything I was told to get the house and now my money was gone. There were other people who had lost money with the same company and Channel 5 News helped them get their money back. I was unable to get my money back because I signed a paper that somehow would not let me get my money back. I was praying to God and I was telling Him that this had to stop. I didn't know what to do because I thought that I did everything the right way. There are a few things that will make you sweat, and money is one of them. Instead of me allowing God to be God and waiting for Him to tell me what to do and allow Him to give me peace, I began brewing over the loss. I was thinking that I would have to start all over to save the money so that I would have a deposit. Truthfully, for me when stuff happens, depending on what it is, I will draw a blank and all my knowledge about what God has told me is gone. If a situation gets hot enough, you will stop and be still. God will get your attention through a tough situation to make you STOP.

    Of course, I cried and cried, I did not know what to do and then God brought the time back to my memory when I was in the car with my grandmother. God asked me, "Do you know why your grandma told you that story about not letting the windows down in the car?"

I said, "No."

Then God said, "Your grandma told you that so that you would think about what was going on around you. You were hot and there was no air coming in and you had enough sense to sit still and be quite so that you could cool off." Instead of me allowing God to be God and waiting for Him to tell me what to do I was fussing and not focusing. God placed an opportunity in my way where I was able to get my house, 3 acres of land in the country just like I prayed for years before. I walked into my house for only $34 dollars. My house had furniture in it and it really blew my mind. The only reason I had to pay the $34 was because something was on my credit. Let's not mention credit, it was not so great; but I was approved.

The enemy's job is to keep us moving so fast that we don't observe our surroundings. We don't use good reasoning and we do not pay attention to details. God wants us to be still and know that He is God. God is aware of all things. It is our reaction that is the catalyst in the situation.

When life becomes too overwhelming, take the time and remember the moments when flashes of lifelines come to help pull you out of tough situations or when lifelines keep you from making mistakes that can be avoided. Now, when things get tough I will think about my grandmother and I get still and listen for what God has to say. Life will teach you through others' wisdom or God-given wisdom. Either way wisdom leads to maturity and growth. I don't know why my grandmother told me that story. Maybe it was because God had to give her that revelation or someone did her like that as a child. I am not sure, but I would love to know.

# JEWEL OF FLASH

Life is the classroom that we attend every day. This classroom of life is moving fast, and we cannot allow it to move so fast that we are moving at a pace that is not for us. We have to take the time to reflect on our day and our life so that when things in life happen, we don't lose ourselves in folly when we know who God is and what He has done.

People will show us flashes or glimpses of who they are. Do not ignore the flashes. People's character shows who they are all the time and we do not want to overlook or give excuses for behavior that is not good for us . When a person flashes with inconsistencies, at some point, the real them will show up. Often times, after the fact, we can see the clues that something was not right, but it will be too late if we have time invested in the person. We should identify them so that we will be able to protect ourselves.

**Jewel of Flash**

The Jewel of Flash is revelation, a moment in time where there is an opportunity to get valuable knowledge that will get us closer to answers that we have been wanting. These moments are nuggets in time and when they come, listen to them and understand their meanings. The Jewel is in the Flash. The Jewel of Flash is connected to discernment. We have to understand the connection of what is going on at that time and what the Flash is trying to tell us.

*Declaration*

Savior, You are the giver of salvation. Lord, I am determined to be submitted under Your will. Lord, my desire is to not allow life disappointments to distract me from Your promise. Your presence is always before me to give me peace that surpasses all understanding. I am determined to arrange myself under Your authority and direction so that I can make quality decisions and prosper in knowledge, wisdom, understanding, finances, friendships and every area in my life. I know there is no need for me to move unless I have a plan to be successful. Amen.

# CHAPTER 5

*The Jewel of Aspiring*

## *Sapphire*

Sapphire is a stone of wisdom and royalty, of prophecy and Divine favor.

Aspire: to want to have or achieve something (such as a particular career or level of success); to seek to attain or accomplish a particular goal.

I have had the pleasure of being around some wonderful women who have helped me aspire to become what God has intended me to become. I thank God all the time for placing me in their company. I have never been the type who was jealous, intimated, or insecure about the intelligence of another woman. I think that it is an opportunity for me to learn. It doesn't matter where I am, whether in the grocery store or some type of social function, if I see a woman and her hair, outfit, or shoes are on point I will walk across the room to tell her, "Girl, you look good. I like your outfit." Or I may ask her, "Did you take your picture today?" If she has not taken her picture, I will take it for her. If she has taken the time to put herself together and look good, I can tell her without any hesitation how good she looks.

I encourage women to always be prepared to take a picture of themselves. When a woman has invested time in getting beautiful she is worthy of being celebrated. Every day is not going to be a good day. Life, circumstances, and the enemy will try to come to steal the promises that God has told her. When those days come, she can always go back and look at those pictures and remember when her faith was strong. When she looks at the pictures, it will help restore the confidence that was lost. A woman should never forget her beauty, who she is, and what her promises are. In the same way, if a woman is intelligent and is able to use her influence to teach me something that I did not know, I can tell her. I will tell her how great the information was and how it impacted me, and sometimes I go as far to ask her, "How did you come up with that?" or "How did she do that?"

We can limit who, where, and what we can be if we don't allow women who are beautiful and powerful to inspire us. How much sense does it make to not take wisdom from someone who is intelligent and who keeps her appearance together because you are insecure? If that is a hang-up for us it needs to change. That is an immature thought process.

## THE JEWEL OF ASPIRING

Would it be better to listen to someone who doesn't know anything? They may get you somewhere, but at a slower pace. We can't allow our feelings to cause us to miss out on information that could change our situation. If we have something good to offer to other women and other women don't want to receive our information or they have a preconceived idea about us, we may think that it was a little immature. Keeping that in mind as we move forward, give other women their props and acknowledge what they can teach us, how they look, and their accomplishments. Many times, if women are not so good at something other women don't have a problem acknowledging that.

Aspiring is changing the atmosphere from the old way broken women did things to the new way that healed, confident women do things. Aspiring and empowering other women is for us to have part ownership in another woman's value. When I say ownership, I mean an investment. When we see her progress, we can see the things that we taught her. It is almost like watching a tree or flower grow that we planted. Although, we are aspiring her, she is still her own person. We cannot dictate her life or act with a resentful spirit because we are helping her become who God has designed her to be.

We have to remember who we are and that we plan to be a mover and a shaker in our gifts and talents. Whatever other women have going on with their gifts and talents are theirs and ours are ours. The more connections, talent, and knowledge that we have, puts us in a place to be a source and resource that causes a bigger network for women to have. If we can embrace these values, we will be that woman who can meet her goals while also aspiring other women to be more.

# THE JEWEL OF ASPIRING

As women we are extravagant. Extravagant is defined as excessively high; exceeding the bounds of reason, as actions demands, opinions or passions; beyond what is deserved or justifiable. I've learned that adoration, deep love and respect follow appreciation when we recognize and enjoy the good qualities in someone or something. We will have full understanding of a situation and we can see that it is bigger than just one woman or thing. When we show another woman love, concern, and affection it makes us feel better to see her smile.

I would not be truthful if I didn't address the behaviors that are in some women. Let's deal with the broken woman. She has wrong motives, she is plotting our demise and trying to get close to us so she can destroy and infect everything that we are working on. This woman will do things that appear to be good gestures. She may give us a gift or say something positive, but truthfully, she is using the synthetic jewels from the enemy. The jewels from the enemy are valuable to his kingdom but they are not valuable in God's Kingdom. Those who use the enemy's jewels have been deceived by the enemy. Unfortunately, there will be women that are like that. These women have severe issues going on that they will have to come face-to-face with.

When our minds do not think deceptive thoughts or think women are dishonest, we will not be thinking in a way that is protective of who we are, and our gifts and we can be easily caught off guard. We can all attest to having met a few of these women in our lifetime. They can't stand you, but they always want to be around you. They are not encouraging and they often throw shade at you when you are successful. These types of women always bring us word of what others have said about us to see if they can get a reaction from us. We have to watch what we say because they are waiting to carry information back. The question we should be asking them is what they said and ask them not to minimize their part.

Listen, if you are friends with someone who is becoming or is successful, they have watched over you, and you have been together for a while, DO NOT allow dumbness to separate you. Unfortunately, some women's capacity cannot withstand the growth of others—even their friends'. Either you are going to progress forward first, or they are. Friends are there to support each other. Is your friendship based on your progress only? You have to know why you are with the people you are with.

If God says move, move. Don't lie on God and say He said move because you are in your feelings of jealousy because they got the deal. If the situation is unhealthy, by all means, move. Continue to pray and hold that position in your friendship. Your sister-friend is moving, but she will need you. She will meet new people and make other connections. Other women will try to align themselves with her; it may be for good, or to harm her. But because you have known her longer, you are her watcher. This is a part of taking that ownership in another woman's value because you are protecting her and being her watchman as she is moving in her purpose. She needs your protection, so she can reach her full value. If the enemy gets you to move out of your position, then her purpose and your purpose can be delayed. The right thing to do is to bring women up as you come up. God is watching. He will make sure that your work and commitment are not in vain.

If you are the woman in the successful position, you must recognize what you have. You should also know the hearts of those who labor among you. The grass may be greener on the other side, but is the taste bitter or sweet? Don't be so consumed with new people or their new ideas, that you forget about the ones who were with you back when things were tough. I see this happening too often; for whatever reason, when women become successful, they change their posse. It may be necessary, but before you do that, be prayerful. There are going to be growing pains and discomfort either way. Friends challenge, encourage, and refresh each other.

I always wanted to have a best friend or someone to be close to who would be ready at the drop of a dime to 'set it off,' if need be. At that time in my life, I had the passion but not the friend. Now this is not to say that I did not have people around me that I hung with, cared about or loved; because I did. It was that what I gave of myself to others, I did not get back. Now I do get back the passion that I give. Back then, I did not get the same satisfaction that I get today with my friend.

When I was younger I always wanted a sister but that never happened so, I desired a best friend. When Brandy, an R&B artist, came out with the song "Best Friend," that was my theme song. However, at that time, I had no one to join me in saying, "That is *our* theme song."

My cousin and I grew up together as little girls and then we went on our separate paths. When we got older and got saved we started hanging again and we became really close. We started sharing war stories, experiences, traveling together, and encouraging each other. God answered my prayer, He gave me my "Best Friend" and that is now our theme song.

Brandy recorded this song in 1994, and I was about 20-years old when it came out. It took almost that same length of time to have a person make me feel like that song made me feel the first time I heard it. The song was so powerful to me.

**"Best Friend"**
Whenever I'm down, I call on you my friend
A helping hand you lend, in my time of need so I
I'm calling you now, just to make it through
What else can I do, don't you hear my please
Friends may come and friends may go
But you should know that
I've got your back, it's automatic
So never hesitate to call
Cuz I'm your sister and always for ya and I

Chorus-I don't know what I'd ever do without you
From the beginning to the end
You've always been here right beside me
So I'll call you my best friend
Through the good times and the bad ones
Whether I lose or If I win
I know one thing that never changes and
That's you as my best friend
Whenever I'm down
With all that's going on, it's really going on Just one of those days
You say the right thing, to keep me moving
To keep me going strong, what else can I say
Friends are there through thick and thin
Well I've been told that
And I believe that it's automatic
Call me when you need a friend
Cuz I'm your sister and always for ya and I don't know

**[REPEAT CHORUS (2x)]**

# THE JEWEL OF ASPIRING

I'll be there for you
When you're going through,
wouldn't you be my friend
Friend you can count on me
Call me when you need me

Do you have a friend like that? Everyone should have at least one. We will need authentic friends to help us stay on track by encouraging us and checking on us. We need friends to get away on vacation with. Friends have boundaries that should be respected.

This is what my best friend Tarsha R. Palmer is like. Every word of this song is true to who she is to me. I can call her and she knows the right thing to say to keep me moving; she never hesitates. Tarsha is quick to set me straight when I am wrong and that is what I love about her. Friends laugh at each other when they do stuff. You have to have someone who allows you to be you. When you need to vent, you need a friend. When you've done something crazy, you need a friend. Accountability breeds responsibility. Accountability and responsibility should work together. Every woman no matter her position in life is equally responsible for the success of the Kingdom. The Kingdom is involved in aspiring women to a greater level in God. In order to reach the goals of the Kingdom we as women have to work together.

Do you have a Best Friend? Does your Best Friend have these qualities? Every girl needs a Best Friend!

**Jewel of Aspire**

The Jewel of Aspire is a gift this Jewel can be worn with any outfit, on any day. The wonderful thing about this Jewel is that it does not have to be kept far from the heart. It

# THE JEWEL OF ASPIRING

should be easy to find a kind word of encouragement for your sister. Believe in someone else besides yourself and see how far they will go.

## *Declaration:*

I will use my Jewel of Aspire to take ownership in my sisters' lives to keep them uplifted. Knowing that my sisters depend on me and I depend on them, I will make sure that I am the best woman that I can be for myself and for them. I own the gifts of kindness, patience, love, confirmation, affirmation, and encouragement. I will share those gifts by telling my sisters what they need to hear, when they need to hear it. I will give hope to women to reach the highest heights in their lives. I vow to not leave a woman with the perception that she has no value, I will help her reshape her view about herself.

# CHAPTER 6

*Jewel of Energy & Growth*

*Quartz*

Quartz enhances spiritual growth, spirituality and wisdom. Because it clarifies thought processes and emotions, it can increase inspiration and creativity.

Growth: a stage in the process of growing: full growth; progressive development; increase, expansion; maturing; a natural process of increasing in size or developing; a gradual increase; something producing and growing.

Spiritual Growth: God promises to stay involved through the lifelong process of spiritual growth.

Philippians1:6 states, "...*being confident of this very thing, that He who has begun a good work in you will complete it until the day of Jesus Christ.*" You have to stay connected with Jesus. In life, you have to stay connected with the right people.

Having the right kind of people around us is very important. Certain types of influences can cause us to act and do things that we would not normally do; spirits and behaviors transfer. Make sure that the people we choose to spend time around are good. This will ensure that the spirits and behaviors that are being transferred by us and them won't affect anyone in a negative way. Always keep in mind, that we didn't bring any bad spirits and we won't take any with us when we leave."

While moving forward, whether our steps are fast or slow, make sure that there is growth. Sometimes in life when the challenges come, and we must make the tough decisions, growth can seem to be at a standstill. This part of life can have us in a holding place for a long time, usually longer than we would like. Growth is set up on principles that have to be followed in ordered for them to work, and at any given stage, the growth can be stunted if something is skipped.

If we don't grow and change in the process of life we will get left behind. Growth is a part of God's process. We start in heaven and He sends us to earth. We are born as babies then we grow in age and knowledge. We are required by law to go to receive an education. If not, the government will step in and arrest the parents for allowing their underage child skip school. In life, if you don't grow and mature in the things of God, the enemy of this world will arrest you and the cost can be severe.

## THE JEWEL OF ENERGY & GROWTH

Grade levels in school start at Pre-K and go through the 12th grade; after which are college and graduate school. Learning can be annoying when you are not interested in the subject and if you think you will not ever use the information in life you may halfway learn it. In high school, college, and graduate school you will learn a lot of information. When you get a job, the first thing they do is provide you with on-the-job training. They will not necessarily do things the way you learned them in school, but you can use the information that you learned to generate new ideas or improve existing standards. We may not want to go to school to learn, but every day that we get up, we are going to school at *Living Life Daily*. There is an automatic enrollment for those who are still breathing. This school is full of lessons, surprise tests, quizzes, drop-outs, and new members. The cost is our survival! The quality of our survival is up to us, this becomes an individual decision. What quality of survival will you have? It is up to you the way you are going to grow. What are you going to do?

You may say I am tired; I am done; I am not doing this thing called life. News flash, you will do life as long as you are breathing. You may not do it well, but you will do it. Not doing life well is ripping women apart. The Bible says in, Romans 15:1-2, *"We who are strong ought to bear with the failings of the weak and not to please ourselves. Each of us should please our neighbors for their good, to build them up."*

We have no other choice but to live life well! If we are not living life well, we may experience such symptoms and/or emotions of feeling down, depressed, crying, calling out for help, or searching for something that is missing. We should not want another woman to experience those emotions and if they do we should have the answer for them so they can be free. Take a minute to think of the worst experience you have ever gone through. Would you want to tell others so that they will not have to feel that pain? We were created to love and nurture one another; we can't do that if we are in pieces all the time.

Have you ever tried to reach out to certain women and they are like cactuses? You reach out to embrace them, but they make it hard. You see the need that they have, and you want to help, but because of the effects of not living life well they can make it hard for other women to get close to them. When other women see them coming they are talking under their breath, "Oh Lord here she comes!" We don't want to be the woman that other women don't want to deal with. Don't be the negative woman; the woman who is always complaining about everybody and everything. Don't be the woman who thinks the whole world is against her. Don't be the woman who NEVER smiles or the woman who only finds joy in other people's sorrows. Don't be the woman of chaos/foolishness.

This is a woman of destruction, a woman stunted in her growth. There is something in her negativity that feeds the sadness in her. Growth takes nurturing. Living life well will fix all this. This is not to say trials won't come, but we will be strong enough to not allow things to stunt us. When those things come up against us it will grow us up to be the phenomenal women that God purposed us to be. We want to be women that other women can come to for reinforcement. The only way to get here is through spiritual, mental, and physical growth.

My pastor, Pastor Andy Thompson, preached a sermon series on making the right choices, Choices: Good, Better, and Best, How Do I Choose and The Most Crucial Choice. In these sermons, he talked about making sure that your chooser is working, and it is not off-kilter.

Off-kilter means not aligned or balanced

**Three Levels of Choices**

*Level 1: Choosing good over evil.*[2] Doing everything in your power to choose good over evil. Even when you break-up with evil it always comes around to try to get back together with you.

*Level 2: Choosing better over good and best over better.*[3] Choosing life over death. In life there are good, better, and best choices but you choose good choices when you could have chosen the best. Learn to test and approve the will of God.

*Level 3: Choosing people for intimacy.*[4] A valuable lesson is choosing the right people. How do you choose the right people for intimacy? In his message, intimacy is not in the context of sexual intimacy; it is used in reference to close, personal relationship with someone. For example:
    a. Not talking about family, you don't have a choice in that, talking about friends, spouse, business partners, people you will love.
    b. Not talking about, 'I love you,' and never see them again, people that you breathe the same air, people you are close to.

We cannot allow a bad choice today to mess-up our tomorrow. If we have survived something and have lived to

---

[2] Pastor Andy Thompson, "Choices; Good, Better, and Best" (sermon, World Overcomers Christian Church, Durham, NC, September 6, 2017).
[3] Pastor Andy Thompson, "How do I Choose?" (sermon, World Overcomers Christian Church, Durham, NC, August 29, 2017).
[4] Pastor Andy Thompson, "The Most Crucial Choice" (sermon, World Overcomers Christian Church, Durham, NC, August 23, 2017)

see another day, consider that a WIN! We have an opportunity to make things better.

You will have to get the series to really get the full impact of it; it is available at: www.worldovercomers.org

In life, you may have chosen the best choice for you at the time because your options were limited. Now that you are reading this book, know that your options are greater than you could have ever imagined. Connecting with other women can add a new perspective to your life. The things that you are trying to achieve, they may have the resources for, or they may be the motivation that you need to keep you moving in the right direction. The same choices that you made about money, relationships, family, children, and business 10 years ago will be different when you are 10 years older.

Have you ever seen a tree growing crooked? For whatever reason, it has gotten out of formation; it looks different and has taken on a different shape. Normally, a tree grows straight, tall, and strong, but when something hinders its growth and causes the tree to bend to the left or right, it still grows but it just looks funny. The tree must adapt to the change, strengthen itself at the bending points, and keep growing.

Can you imagine the pain that the tree has to go through because it is out of its formation? In the genetics of the tree, it is set for the tree to grow straight up. The tree still found a way to continue to grow because that is its true nature; to grow straight in the air. Life can cause you to get out of formation and take on a different shape. Allow the pains to form a better you, a happier you, a stronger you, and an empowered you. I did not say that the tree was less beautiful because it was growing crooked. Life will demand energy from you. Whether you use the energy for good or bad, the demand will be there.

We are quick to judge a person when they do something that makes no sense. Well, it makes absolutely no sense to get up every day and not do anything productive. The energy and time that we waste on unproductive things could be used to get us ahead. We make a choice to be wasteful and then we are disappointed because our outcome wasn't something better. Connecting with productive women will generate the right energy and cause us to plunge ourselves into places we may not normally go because our energy was not wasted.

If you notice groups of women, there is always a mixture of energy such as, outgoing/talkative, shy, smart, OCD, carefree, the comedian, the prissy one, and the one who is ready to fight all the time. This is good energy because they all will compliment each other, and the energy will keep everyone moving. Will they have disagreements? Yes, because all of them are good at their own thing and they can help the ones that are not so good at it. Then when a new 'girl movie' comes out, they are trying to find their character in the movie. Their friends have to point out to them how they are acting, and they can laugh and have fun.

Pray that God places women full of positive energy in your circle.

**Jewel of Energy and Growth**

Growth is something that your Jewel needs to stay effective. Living a life without growth is living life at a minimum. When you are bound, you are incomplete and those around you are growing and moving on. Take your

Jewel, get in some of that old fertilizer that life has dealt you and GROW!

*Declaration:*

I purpose in my heart today that the delay in my growth is over. My energy levels will increase, and I will become motivated to do the work in me so that it will work for my good. My growth has been stunted and I have been allowing life to pass me by and slip away. I owe it to myself to use my Jewel of Growth to grow up and mature in to the woman God has called me to be. God redeem the time for me. Forgive me for my slothfulness.

# CHAPTER 7

*Jewel of Wisdom*

*Jacinth*

Jacinth is the wisdom of discernment. The virtue is able to impart wisdom to the immature as well as the mature.

Wisdom: ability to discern inner qualities and relationships; good sense; knowledge that is gained by having many experiences in life.

With wisdom, all things are possible. God asked Solomon, "What do you want Me to do for you?" If God asked Solomon this question, do you believe that you would have the opportunity to have the same question asked to you by God? Would your answer be wisdom, or would it be money or things?

I Kings 3:5-15 says, *"At Gibeon the Lord appeared to Solomon during the night in a dream, and God said, "Ask for whatever you want me to give you." Solomon answered, "You have shown great kindness to your servant, my father David, because he was faithful to you and righteous and upright in heart. You have continued this great kindness to him and have given him a son to sit on his throne this very day. Now, Lord my God, you have made your servant king in place of my father David. But I am only a little child and do not know how to carry out my duties. Your servant is here among the people you have chosen, a great people, too numerous to count or number. So, give your servant a discerning heart to govern your people and to distinguish between right and wrong. For who is able to govern this great people of yours?" The Lord was pleased that Solomon had asked for this. So, God said to him, "Since you have asked for this and not for long life or wealth for yourself, nor have asked for the death of your enemies but for discernment in administering justice, I will do what you have asked. I will give you a wise and discerning heart, so that there will never have been anyone like you, nor will there ever be. Moreover, I will give you what you have not asked for both wealth and honor so that in your lifetime you will have no equal among kings. And if you walk in obedience to me and keep my decrees and commands as David your father did, I will give you a long life." Then Solomon awoke, and he realized it had been a dream. He returned to Jerusalem, stood before the ark of the Lord's covenant and sacrificed burnt offerings and fellowship offerings. Then he gave a feast for all his court."*

II Corinthians 2:11 says, *"lest Satan should get an advantage of us, for we are not ignorant of his devices."*

# JEWEL OF WISDOM

I am aware that I have heard some things about myself. I am aware that I have been judged, talked about, lied on, cheated on, and even misused. These are just a few things that I can say that I am aware of. I just wanted you to know when you become enlightened to wisdom it will take you to another level of awareness. The reason why I picked the negative things to say is because these types of things seem to hinder our movement towards God and living life. When our feelings get hurt we feel like retaliation or vengeance needs to happen. But I tell you, this is the time for us to use wisdom and know ourselves. We have to be aware of the things that we used to do such as going to parties, doing drugs, and drinking, and the penalties that we endured because of them. We have to be aware of the dudes we were with and what we did with them. We must also be aware of the hurt we endured, the tears we cried and the length of time it took for us to get them out of our minds and our hearts.

Wisdom will allow us to stand strong no matter what we have been through. Wisdom lets us know that we are forgiven by God. Wisdom will remind us and allow us to reflect on the things that caused us pain or hindered us in life. Proverbs 4:6 says *"Do not forsake wisdom, and she will protect you; love her, and she will watch over you. The beginning of wisdom is this: Get wisdom. Though it cost all you have, get understanding."*

Wisdom will stand guard to protect us by giving us instructions on how to avoid those dangerous pitfalls. Wisdom should be so loud that when the old foolishness shows up, we should be moving in the other direction.

Have you ever been standing somewhere and a dude comes walking towards you and you can read him from a distance? Or have ever tried to make a business deal and the other person starts talking and in your mind you say, "Here we go." Why? Because you have dealt with these types of people before and wisdom is telling you to beware. If you find yourself as a repeat offender, you need a good support system. Some days, when you get off work, you drive home and you don't even remember doing it because it is a habit. If you are falling for the same sins, setbacks, downfalls, or into the same pits, it is time to do self-evaluation. You may not be able to do the evaluation on yourself; you might need to get help.

Now this is real talk. We know if we want to change and stop doing something, we will begin to talk about it and start taking steps to change our behavior. The worst thing is to get others tied up in our mess knowing we are not ready to change. People are willing to help us but we must be sincere in our request. Their time is precious.

We as women have to realize that no matter where we are in our strength, we have to be able to carry our own weight at some point. We cannot be victims all our lives, needing assistance in everything we do. No one should have to hold our hand all the time because they have other things to do too. There is a real need in this world and it's time-out for the foolishness. That spirit needs to be called out and dealt with so we all can move on.

There is a difference in wanting help and wanting attention. Have you ever known someone who knew that what they were doing was wrong and they asked everybody they knew what they thought? All the while, they were trying to find someone to agree with their logic, so they would feel better and keep doing what they knew was wrong. A fool will give foolish advice. We are at a pivotal moment in time when we have turned the tables on the enemy and have taken back our mindset, our will power, and the desire to live a quality life. Sugar can't be put on everything and you can't expect your foolishness to be accepted in this important time.

As I have gotten older, I have learned something new every day. Wisdom is infinite. Have you ever wanted something so bad because of what you knew about it at that time; but as time went on and you learned more or learned of more options you changed your mind about wanting that thing? As we grow in maturity, we become cautious about things. When making decisions, we will think and wait on wisdom to help us make the right choices.

I can remember when I wanted someone so bad that I knew it was not good, but my truth and love were distorted. I did not have faith for someone better; my clarity was not clear, and wisdom was absent. Let me say this, wisdom was there, I just chose not to listen to it. See, I have to be honest too. I knew to do right, but I chose not to and then I went into denial. That is the state of mind that I was in then. It takes two to make a thing go bad. I will not act like the victim because I did a lot too. I just refused to let go of someone that I knew was bad. I would not go anywhere because I wanted to try to stick it out to see if I could make it work. But we all know we cannot make anyone stay if they do not want to stay.

If you are in a situation where you are trying to make someone stay, really consider it and get some help. I do not want to elaborate on something without knowing the details of your situation but talk to someone who is trustworthy and has a good reputation. Long story short, he left me and it hurt; it hurt badly and the pain went deep. I prayed for my sanity and I prayed that the Lord would make me better and not bitter. I began to seek wisdom because I needed something good to help me cover the bad.

This relationship happened for some years, so this was not the first breakup, but this was the last. I had to choose wisdom and let go and walk away. He called, and I could have taken him back, but I had enough and there was nothing else to talk about. My understanding is, if it's over then it's over. There had been enough vocabulary words expressed between the two of us. What could I have possibly said that he hadn't heard me say already?

Don't allow your tolerance level to get so used to the abnormal that you consider it to be normal. You have to know when enough is enough for you. The best thing he could have done was to walk out that rainy night. Even though it was raining outside that night, the sun was beginning to shine. My life was just beginning. The process was hard, but I pushed my way through it. Don't get upset with the rain because it serves it purpose. Rain is needed to make things grow.

Don't only seek wisdom to cover the bad, seek wisdom to cover the good too. Again, wisdom is infinite. I can say I was glad, ecstatic, super excited when wisdom showed up and I opened up to receive it. Another lesson in life is to embrace wisdom when she shows up. Accept the truth about what she tells you because wisdom can be your best friend.

Proverbs 4:5-7 states, *"Get wisdom, get understanding; do not forget my words or turn away from them. Do not forsake wisdom, and she will protect you; love her, and she will watch over you. The beginning of wisdom is this: Get wisdom. Though it cost all you have, get understanding."*

**Jewel of Wisdom**

Wisdom is the Jewel that you should have polished at all times in your jewelry box. Wisdom is the guard of all the Jewels because wisdom knows what the other Jewels don't know. Wisdom is standing guard protecting it all. Listen to wisdom when she speaks so that no one can come and steal your Jewels or plant a fake jewel in your box that may cause your other Jewels to tarnish.

***Declaration:***

I walk with my friend Wisdom because she has knowledge that I do not have. Wisdom has never let me down and even when I forsake her, Wisdom stands by me ready to shield me from any harm that may come my way. I will use the Jewel of Wisdom to help me heal from any pains that foolishness, ignorance and inexperience caused me. Today I will respect Wisdom and be careful not to neglect her as I go through life because I will always need her. Wisdom is my companion that will walk with me all the days of my life.

# Chapter 8

*Jewel of Balance*

*Agate*

Agate promotes inner stability, composure, and maturity. Its warm, protective properties encourage security and self-confidence.

Balance: the ability to move or to remain in a position without losing control or falling; a state in which different things occur in equal or proper amounts or have an equal or proper amount of importance.

Balance is the center of things. Equilibrium is the part of your balance system that provides your brain with information about changes in head movement with respect

## JEWEL OF BALANCE

to the pull of gravity. Balance is keeping who you are at all times and not allowing the circumstances that happen in life to change your balance. Balance is one of the key factors to victory or failure. Balance is not just for a particular people or people with great personalities, bank accounts, good vernacular, and great health. Balance is for everyone. There is warfare for balance in your life. Being unbalanced causes so many underlying issues that will leave important things overlooked. Being unbalanced causes issues, whatever is wrong or whatever the lack, to take precedence over everything.

If we are in a vulnerable place and we are not balanced in who we are or where we are going, that can be the point that causes a lot of time lost. Win or lose, it will depend on us understanding our balance and what we are balancing. If we are consciously ignorant to the value of the Jewel of Balance, we will invite the enemy to come sit at our table. Unresolved balance makes way for the devil to operate and cause chaos in our life. Our mindset will trap us into poor performance and carelessness. Before we know it, our lack of attention will cause us to forget things that are important and cause us to focus on things that are not productive.

Let's choose to simplify the balance battle we face today. Walk freely and fully on the path that we are destined for. If we are expecting company at our house, the first thing we will do is start grabbing the big things to put them away so that the visitors don't see that we had a mess in our house. Less obvious are all the little things that are out of place. The little things can become bigger than the big things.

Let's not forget the small things when balancing our lives. It's about being equipped to balance all things so that we will be influential daily. The alternative is to stay overwhelmed by not doing anything, not knowing where to start, or by thinking we don't have what it takes to get to a balanced life. Which choice is the best choice? Hopefully, none. Is balance a big deal? Yes. Can it make us feel overwhelmed? Sometimes. We can't allow our minds to think for one minute that we can't do it. We are equipped with the Jewel of Balance. Although it may need a little polishing, we have it. We have everything that we need to prevail. We have the capacity to deal with every situation and circumstance that people, finances, jobs, and the devil throw our way. Balance requires control. We have to be attuned to when we are vulnerable so that we stay self-controlled.

The philosophy for our church, which I have adopted into my life, is: *"Balanced Victory for a God Designed Life."* Every time I hear this philosophy, or read it in the lobby of our church, it makes me think of the victories that I have achieved. Some victories were easy and quick, while others required more effort. I got some bruises and I didn't think I was going to make it. Some people may say, "A win is a win." That's true but is there is another way to look at it.

When I think of *Balanced Victory*, I think of the quality of my win. Have you ever gone through something and you were so exhausted that you could not enjoy the victory or the victory was no longer significant? As I have gotten older and learned things along the way in life, I want to apply those things to my Jewel of Balance to ensure that the quality of my wins are good. From the perspective of the quality of the win, we should make sure that our balance is strong and level so that our wins are good wins.

Let's take advantage of experience and education and not just slide in, or barely make it in, on a win; let's win BIG! When we educate ourselves on things that we are involved in such as our relationships, health, job, and finances we will know what is going on. If we are feeling depleted, we should ask ourselves if we have talked to God, prayed, read our Bible or praised. He can, and will, give us all the insight that we need to all our questions.

When my Pastor introduced the phrase, "Balanced Victory for a God Designed Life," I quoted it until it became part of my soul. That phrase moved my Jewels and they unearthed themselves and I began to live in my wins and even when I lost, I won; my balance was not shifted through the process.

The quality of our loss is just as important because when we lose, and there will be times that we will lose, we need to have a perspective that will allow us to see beyond the loss or disappointment.

Hopefully, we will understand the loss and be better prepared the next time. We have to be able to take a loss and be functional. Devastation is a loss that can impair us and can kill us if we are in a vulnerable place.

One of the pivotal things that changed my Balance was a job that I had. I did not realize that this was the opportunity that was presenting itself. I was working at a job that I loved. It was demanding but I really loved the challenges and the things that I learned.

I was a team leader at a car manufacturing company and I worked with the Japanese making transmissions. I can say some days were hard, but I cared about the work I did. Over time, as things began to shift, I did not like going to work as much as I used to. But I was still determined to go and do my best because I knew better was coming. I had been praying to the Lord about my future. Leading up to that moment I was so unhappy and miserable at that job, but because I was so committed, I thought I did not have any other options. This caused my Balance to be off.

Fear is not a part of Balance. I was fearful of starting over and fearful of the unknown. I am a person who is consistent, and I believe in longevity at jobs. I wanted to complete my bachelor's degree and start my own business, but I couldn't because that job took up so much of my time. I was working 12- to 13-hour days and the things that I dreamed of doing could not fit into the hours of my job. I used to tell my coworker, "I am going to be a millionaire. This right here ain't it." She laughed and told me to not forget about her.

When it got to the point that management wanted to devalue who I was because I refused to allow them to place fault on me for something I did not do, I walked away. At that point I had to decide whether I valued myself enough to walk away. The Jewel of Balance leveled herself! I knew that I worked hard at that company and if anyone were to ask people at the company they would tell them the same thing. If they did not care or believe in me, which they did not, why should I stay? That was exactly what I needed to leave.

Let me be clear, we cannot walk away from every tough situation, but sometimes that is the motivation that we need to get us moving. This is where the Jewel of Balance comes in. I had to have Balance of who I was and whose I was. God had already told me what was going to happen and I got confirmation from Him when I asked Him, "Can I quit?" He said, "Yes."

Make no mistake about it, I fully trust in God. Balance does not always give us answers. There were days that I asked God if He *really* told me to leave? I had to go and check my Balance because Balance cannot waiver.

Balance will always leave the spectator in awe and his/her mouth open in disbelief, but it is okay. The confidence that accompanies our Balance will allow us to walk with your head up. We do not have to defend ourselves against the decisions that we make when God and Balance is aligning our lives with destiny. Things will happen in our lives so that Balance can have its perfect work in our lives. When things seem like they are unfair and when our value is not being seen Balance will move so that we will get all that is meant for us have.

For something that I thought was a little situation, God has taken this to a place that I never could have imagined. Who would have ever thought somebody like me with a jacked-up past like I have could ever achieve the things that I have achieved? Who would have thought that I would have been to the places that I have been, or even been in the company of some of the most talented, anointed, and powerful people ever? Yes, I have…and I did…I am…and guess what? I am not done yet because my possibilities are endless.

We have to understand that we can be in the will of God and all hell can still break loose. We have to know who God is. When we encounter mishap after mishap or when life seems unfair, we cannot allow ourselves or people to make us think that we have sinned, and we are not in right-standing with God. God is in His creative mode and He will work out everything for our good. He is building something that will be able to stay Balanced through any attack, test, or persecution.

**Jewel of Balance**

When things align with Balance, obstacles will not seem to be impossible or overwhelming. Balance allows for clarity and gives a plan to accomplish great things and win. If loss happens, the Jewel of Balance gives nuggets that turn it into a positive loss.

*Declaration*

Today I decree my day as a new day with the Jewel of Balance. I will walk in Balance in every area of my life and nothing will be lacking. Balance is a part of my life that allows me to function as the best me I can be. I will live the best me and my life will reflect it. There is no situation or circumstance that can overtake me, or allow me to perform beneath who God say that I am.

# CHAPTER 9

*The Jewel of Healing*

*Amethyst*

　　Amethyst is based on the stone's ancient reputation for preventing drunkenness, which was perhaps sympathetic magic suggested by its wine like color. People wore the rings before they drank wine.

　　Healing: to make healthy, whole, or sound; restore to health; free from ailment; to bring to an end or conclusion, as conflicts between people or groups, usually with the strong implication of restoring former amity; settle; reconcile; to free from evil; cleanse; purify

## THE JEWEL OF HEALING

When we are being healed there will be times when we will have to move like a chameleon and change with the situation. Something happened but we still have to move as if nothing has happened, changing and blending-in with the scenery as we go. We all go through things, but we cannot allow those things to incapacitate us. We have to keep moving through it.

When we are healed it is an announcement to our inner selves, as well as to the enemy and the world. We need a good confession. "I am not disabled, nor am I a victim or victimized anymore. I will not allow the scandal of this to haunt me, and my name is not scandalized in the Heavens. I couldn't care less what hell thinks. I am not forgotten as though I did not exist, and I will not be ignored or cast aside because of my brokenness. I am healed."

We have to own our healing; it is a process. We will not wake up the day after heartbreak and be totally healed, but we can wake up and start walking in that healing of forgiveness to ourselves and others. We must have some good stored up so that no matter what comes—whether it be death, heartache, or heartbreak—we can still move forward and function. When people are found not functioning at all, usually it has come from a buildup of things and no maintenance.

Being healed is to learn to embrace ourselves because we are not our own enemy. However, if we neglect ourselves long enough we can turn on ourselves and begin to think we are the enemy. Sometimes in life we will spend a lot of time battling "self." Have you ever done something or made a decision that left a residue that lasted a long time and you told yourself, "I was so dumb!" "What was I thinking?" "Why didn't I see it?" or "How could I let that happen?"

# THE JEWEL OF HEALING

Back in the days when I was focused on a life of fun, I would hang out at my Aunt Mae's house. My aunt is a woman of God and she always told me what was right, but at that time I was not trying to hear what she or anyone else was saying. I thought I knew what was best for me. I was young and thought I had time.

One day, my cousin and I were sitting by the clothesline smoking a blunt and drinking Coronas. When my brother David and sister-in-law drove up, I started saying, "Don't come over here with that Jesus stuff." Of course, my vocabulary was very different back then and my statement included profanity. My brother is like a walking Bible, quoting scriptures and correcting you if you said it wrong.

David walked over to where I was sitting and began to prophesy to me. He said this to me, "I see you on a stage in front of a lot of people speaking; there are so many people."

I looked at him and said, "How in the world am I going to be on stage and I am not even saved yet?" Only, again my statement included profanity; I didn't actually say 'world.' My brother just looked at me; he did not say anything else, then he walked away. I was mad and my high was gone. I was quickly sober and there were no effects that I had even been getting high. The power and authority of God that my brother was walking in took all that away. I could not get high anymore more that day because all I could hear was his voice playing back in my head.

It was not that the drugs and alcohol were not working, it was what he said had hit the Jewel that was planted inside my soul from the beginning of time. The "self" that I know now would not have dared to speak like that about Jesus, I had to be healed from that bad place. Jesus hung on the cross and looked down through time and saw me sitting at the clothesline in all my ignorance and said, "Father forgive her, she know not what she does." If no one else can identify and be grateful for Jesus hanging on the cross, I can.

We have to be healed from that old "self" and walk in our new self. I look back on this story and I praise God as though I just got saved for the first time all over again. In this moment, He allowed me to have this memory to remind me that even though it was not my greatest moment it had much value. The Jewel that was in me pressed and formed and now, many years later, I can walk in that prophecy.

When the enemy placed the synthetic jewel of bondage on my neck, I became enslaved to it; it began damaging my mind, body, and soul. God had a plan and turned it around in my favor. I did not take heed at that time what the enemy was doing and the effect it was having on my life. But the seed of life had been planted, the Jewel was revealed, and I thought of what my brother said to me often.

The enemy was there, and he heard what I heard so he tried to keep me tangled up in sin so that I couldn't start walking in the calling that God had for me. But grace and mercy were covering me. As I looked back over life, some moments were unknown and hard, I wondered why me? Why did I have to be the one to go down this path? For a long time, I wrestled with why. I always asked God why I wasn't like my cousins who went to church. I figured that maybe I would not have gone through this.

It would be really nice if we could pick all the right things in life. Even if we did, there is still an adversary, the devil, who is going back and forth to see who he can deceive and devour. In order to really appreciate who God is, He will

## THE JEWEL OF HEALING

have to rescue and redeem us from some situations so that we know that His love is real. If God did not love us, He would have left us to our own thinking.

As we all know, everyone has their own cross to bear. Jesus carried His cross and hung on it; we are called to do the same. Matthew 16:24 states, *"Then Jesus said to his disciples, 'Whoever wants to be my disciple must deny themselves and take up their cross and follow me.'"* Comparing our lives with others' is not the thing to do. Whatever our cross is, pick it up because we are equipped to carry it. Jesus hung on the cross for humanity; for our sins that He did not commit. Each of our crosses may require us to do the same.

I was asking God over and over what was wrong with me. Why don't I ever fit in? Everywhere I went, I never felt that I fit in. Even when I did drugs, I felt out of place. One Sunday when I went to church my uncle, Pastor Williams told me, "You keep asking God what is wrong with you. He said nothing is wrong with you. You did not fit in because He did not want you to fit in." We have to be all right with the seasons when we do not fit in, these are growing and healing seasons. We shouldn't force who we are on people who can't accept who we are, even if we don't fully understand who we are becoming.

All through those dark places, God had me covered. Although I was doing drugs and trying to fit in with people, He covered me so that I would become who He wanted me to become and not crossbred with anything that would taint what He was doing in me and through me.

My grandmother used to put her index finger on people with a little force, push her finger down, and tell them "Get in your place." She always told me that and I did not know where my place was, but today I can say, "Grandma, I found my place."

I always had a heart to share, give, and help people. Because of the things that I went through and because I was treated like I was treated, it could have made me not want to be a giving person who did positive things; but it only made me want to do it more. I had an identity problem and God was beginning to reveal to me who I was in Him. God does not reveal purpose by sending a letter with all the details, although it would be a lot easier and less frustrating. He used my experiences to guide me down a customized path. His picture is much bigger, and the outcome is greater than we can imagine.

Some people learn their purpose early in life and others learn their purpose later. I had to understand and consider that either way, God allows me to be in certain places in my life or He puts me there for reasons only He knows. I had to get healed from those places where I thought that I was robbed of life when I was doing bad and everyone else was doing good. I was the cousin everyone talked about; they always had something negative to say about me. Out of all the group of cousins who did drugs and hung out, my name always made the top two. I never lost my place on the billboard. Once I was able to understand what God was doing in me, I realized that I had a strength that only that process could have given me.

I may not ever know the impact that my life has on others, but if one person can be changed, saved, or made better then I will say it was worth it. Some things in life will not be pleasant and we have to be able to take it. This is a world where only the strong will survive. There are a few things that I don't need anyone to tell me; one of them is that I have strength. When the enemy whips on us the right way and we make it through, win or lose we can look that devil in his face and tell him, "Try it again! I will not go down like that again!"

That is the awesome thing about healing. If you break a bone, cut your finger, or fall and bruise yourself, your body will begin to heal itself on its own because that is how God designed it. When things happen in our lives that we have done to ourselves or if others have done it to us, our body will go into healing mode. The thing that keeps us from healing is, *us*. If we relive the events and keep talking about them that keeps the pain open and fresh and prevents the healing process.

When we are first injured, that is when it is most painful. Even though the healing part can be painful too because the wound is sore, it can start to itch and grow a scab. If we slammed our finger in a door right now and it cracked a fingernail, it would hurt, and we would cry and scream, or whatever we do when we are hurt. As time goes by our finger starts to heal, it will be sore and bruised. When our finger is almost healed it would be crazy to put that finger back in the door and slam it again because we know it going to hurt. But this is how we can be when it comes to healing from hurt and loss.

I am by no means minimizing any hurt, pain or loss that we may have been through; however, I know that in this world all types of things have happened to people. It is to say that we must find a way to heal and move on. We cannot slam that same finger in a door every day, every week, every month or every year. If we do, we are going to lose that finger and possibly our hand because the infection of the wound will spread and affect other parts of our body.

The body is made to repair itself but if we keep traumatizing it, the body will go into shock. The symptoms of shock include: cold and sweaty skin, pale or grey skin, rapid pulse, irregular breathing, dizziness, fatigue, dilated pupils, and confusion to name a few. There are different types of shock, which include, but are not limited to, infections, low blood pressure, allergic reaction, or massive heart attack. If left untreated, shock is usually fatal. Shock can be treated depending on the cause. Our shock may not literally kill us, but it can kill the healing process that enables us to have a productive life for ourselves and our families, and our destiny. These are the symptoms of living with shock: sadness, unhappiness, isolation, victimization, angry, lack of peace, lack of joy, and darkness where we attempt to hide hoping that no one can see us. Given the proper conditions we can live in this world and be dead to life.

**Jewel of Healing**

Disappointment, hurt, and loss rob us of the Jewel that is designed to heal the body, mind and soul. The Jewel of Healing is restoration to the body that fights off any imbalances and anything that goes against God's perfect will for our life.

*Declaration:*

Everything and every place that is within me that is not healed, I call it healed. I break the bonds of brokenness so that every area in my life is healed and made whole. The thoughts that I have about my process and my past will change because I know that all things will work for my good because I am called for the purposes of God and I do believe what God has said about me.

# CHAPTER 10

*The Jewel of Truth*

*Chrysolite*

Chrysolite is also known as Peridot, stone of detoxification, purification. Bringing us a feeling of liberation.

Truth: the real facts about something; the things that are true; the quality or state of being true; a statement or idea that is true or accepted as true

Don't let people write your future for you based on their assumptions or your past, and don't write your future based on your past, or what you think. Your truth should be what God thinks; He has written your life story.

# THE JEWEL OF TRUTH

It's okay to have questions. Sometimes you need to doubt. Sometimes you need to question. In fact, a lot of times uncertainty is the foundation that will allow dreams, purpose, and destiny grow.

When I was about 11 or 12, I was spending time at my grandmother's house and all my aunts, uncles, and cousins were sitting around talking about God. I just said, "Well who put Him in charge and why do it have to be His way?" The room got silent and everyone looked at me. There was almost a funeral that day and it would have been mine.

They were saying, "You don't question God! That's not your place!" I did not know, I was just asking and to me, it was just a simple question. So, from that day I was always scared to ask God anything because of the response that they gave me. But thank God, He came and gave me a clearer understanding.

On my father's side of the family they went to church; the Church of God in Christ (COGIC); on my mother's side they did not go to church regularly and they partied on weekends. I saw two different worlds and I was trying to piece this thing together because it did not make sense to me.

When I was at my Grandma Jewel's house, I went to church. But when I went home, I was in a different atmosphere, so I changed to fit my surroundings. If we struggle with doubt or have genuine questions, we shouldn't panic or feel reluctant to seek the truth. If we are sincerely looking for answers, God will meet us, and faith will spring from the answers we find. There will be some questions that we will not get the answers for in this lifetime. Keep pursuing righteousness and everything will work out.

# THE JEWEL OF TRUTH

Are we willing to see the reflection of ourselves regardless of our feelings? Are we willing to pay the price? Are we willing to accept 100% responsibility for truth about who we are, be it good or bad? Are we willing to get the counseling or mentoring that we may need to overcome things that are hindering us?

The fact of the matter is that in order to be successful, we have to know who we are. When we know who we are, our success will take sacrifice and hard work. It will require us to be resolved in our mind so that we will be true to who we are, no matter what. We will have to understand what type of person we want to be. Many people are true to themselves, but they are not the most honest, sincere, or loveable people, and they are okay with that. We have to know what type of person we want to be and stick to it. The ultimate test to see if we are really true to ourselves is to reflect on our response when someone says or does something wrong to us . Will we stay true to our genuine self? Will we still be that loving caring person? We all know when the right buttons are pushed how we can react.

In 1 Peter 3:15, it says, *"But in your hearts revere Christ as Lord. Always be prepared to give an answer to everyone who asks you to give the reason for the hope that you have. But do this with gentleness and respect, keeping a clear conscience, so that those who speak maliciously against your good behavior in Christ may be ashamed of their slander. For it is better, if it is God's will, to suffer for doing good than for doing evil."* Your hope is to please God and to show the world there is a higher power that works in you.

My pastor always says, "You do right because right is right to do. You don't do right only because *they* do right or because you are being watched." Clearly, this is big pill to swallow but it is so true. That statement has kept me from snatching the breath out of some people. Especially, when they are trying to test me. You have to recognize this trait in people because it can be to your advantage to be proactive.

One day my aunt was having a cookout at her house so me, my son, and other family members went there. The conversation came up about drug addiction. My uncle just got out of jail for drug-related issues. I am comfortable talking about it because it does not bother me; that is my truth and the truth of it is, "I am free and delivered!" It is not a bondage that I still wrestle with.

The children were playing really close, and children always have an instinct to want to be in grown-folk's business. I noticed my son stopped playing and he was listening. I noticed that my aunt kept asking questions like, "How did it make you feel and why did you do it? And then she said, "Oh, DeMarquis is listening."

I said, "It's okay because I have already told him about me, my drug addiction, and my selling drugs." Then I looked at my son and said, "DeMarquis, I told you about my drug addiction and that I sold drugs?"

He said, "Yeah, ma you did," and went back to playing. I had to let the enemy know. This is why I called my son by his name and restated the sentence so that he could answer it for himself. This also taught him how to answer people when they said something about me. He should not be scared to share my truth, because I am not scared of my truth.

I did not even entertain whether she was trying to be funny or hurtful because I was free. The truth was, I told my son for that exact reason. I had to make him aware of my past so that he would not repeat what I did. We have to be so true with ourselves, about ourselves, and what we did, because people in their ignorance, insecurities, or efforts to be hurtful and destroy our progress will do and say stuff to cause our setback. We cannot go into a place where we call out their past because they called something out about our past. Sometimes people are genuine in wanting to know how we were able to conquer such a big giant. The thing that we went through may have been tough for them. A friend or loved one may need our knowledge so they can help themselves or someone else.

Being offended and taking things personally can hurt our victory and our freedom. When people ask us about our past and our deliverance, we have to be confident in our answers and reactions. What is the point of going through all that, if no one ever knows? That is our testimony. If we shared it, maybe people would understand who we are and why we are the way we are. A person's personality is connected with their past.

Another truth is, don't be so caught up in trying to figure out everyone's motives. That is a full-time job and we don't have time for that. Our full-time job is to be solid in the person that we are. Irrelevant people should not consume our thoughts or have that much access to us. If they are consuming our thoughts and our life, the truth is we are not free.

When I first changed my life, people quite often wanted to tell me who I used to be and what I used to do. They would say things like, "I remember when you used to do this or that." In my mind, I am thinking, 'You knew me back then and you feel safe enough to come to me and tell me,' but because I had changed and was saved by grace my reaction was not the one that they thought. I agreed and said, "Look at me now!"

# THE JEWEL OF TRUTH

Because their intentions were wrong, they were left looking like the fool. People love to try to stir us up not knowing the danger they were in. If they did, they would just congratulate us on our progress and let us go on our way. But if we have the opportunity to have some people come to us and try to give us a history lesson about us, give praise of how far we have come. We have to be just as comfortable with the bad as well as the good.

No, I am not proud of all my actions, but it is what it is, and it was what it was. When there are things in our life that will affect the people that we love we need to tell them. If it is painful or hurtful, it will be better if they heard it from us than from someone else. No matter how much we try to hide it, the enemy will find a way to get that information out. That is what bad news does; it won't rest until it has walked here and there to see who will listen. The truth will set us free. The truth is, we have made it through whatever it was, we could have lost our mind or been dead. So, rejoice and allow the truth that God spared us to redeem us to greatness.

What was meant to take us out is going to take us up. The only thing that will hold us in a place of falsehood and shame is giving the power to the enemy and allowing him to hold the truth. If what we did is true, then why should the enemy have that power? The power is ours. The experience is ours. We did it, therefore, the power of that belongs to us and only us. We have to sucker punch the enemy before he can sucker punch us.

Can you imagine the enemy's face that day when I confronted him with the truth that I knew was true and boldly owned it without hesitation? The enemy had to take several seats.

# THE JEWEL OF TRUTH

**Jewel of Truth**

The Jewel of Truth is the Tylenol, Aleve or Advil that will remove the aches and pains that live on or imposes itself on. When you need sleep, peace, or relaxation, take a dose of truth. Truth may need to be taken in moderation if you are not familiar with it, because it can have shocking and hard side effects, but the results will be better for you.

***Declaration:***

I am seeking and invite the Jewel of Truth into my life to expose all fiction, denial, or fabrication about myself. I accept the truth and I am willing to change anything that is found in me that is not pleasing so that my truth will be positive and productive to my life. The truth is I am grateful for this moment that I can admit I have struggled with talking about things in my past with people but today fear will not hold me from owning what I did. I am free to tell the world what God has done for me.

# CHAPTER 11

## *The Jewel of Power*

### *Onyx*

Onyx is thought to have protective properties and to bring inner strength, self-confidence and mental discipline, will power.

Power: having great power, prestige, or influence; leading to many or important deductions; having the ability to control or influence people or things; having a strong effect on someone or something; having or producing a lot of physical strength or force.

# THE JEWEL OF POWER

Have you ever wanted something to eat and there was only one place that you wanted it from? Have you ever been to a drive-thru and you were in a hurry, but you were hungry for a specific thing and this place was the only place that had it and you did not want to go inside? Your mouth could taste it even though you did not have it yet and you could remember the last time you had it and it was so good. This is the same thing that happens when you are waiting on something from God.

Imagine that today you pull up to Burger King where you can 'Have it your way.' You pull up to the drive-thru because you do not want to get out of your car. It is a little busy, but you want this burger and you decide to wait. The cashier asks, "What would you like?" you tell her, and she says, "That will be $8.56. Drive to the first window to pay."

Things are moving along fairly quickly until you get to the second window to pick up your order and the cashier tells you that your order is not ready. She then asks you to pull up and they will bring it out to you when it is ready. Now you get a little irritated because as you pull up you see another car waiting in front of you. When you look in the rearview mirror the line behind you is getting longer. Time is passing, and you begin to look around to see if you can see anyone coming to bring you your order, but no one is coming. As you are still waiting another car pulls up behind you waiting for their special order and now you are saying to yourself, "What is going on and why are they so slow?" Then you start complaining, "This is why I don't like coming over here. This place makes me sick. They need to hire some more people. This doesn't make any sense to make people wait this long, Umph!"

The drive-thru traffic is moving steadily, but your order has not come out. At this point you are annoyed, you

# THE JEWEL OF POWER

want to leave but you have paid for the food and you want it. You don't have time to stop anywhere else, so you have to sit there and wait. How a person regards life, promise, or expectations for themselves reflects how they will receive their order. Are you putting things in jeopardy? There will be powerful times in your life where you can have one of three responses:

1. Order, Pull Up, Grab, and Go.
2. Order, Pull Up, Check, and Go.
3. Order, Pull Up, and Wait.

When you are in this walk called life, there will be times when you have special orders that you want from God and out of life, you will have to decide out of the three how you will receive your order. The *Order, Pull Up, Grab, and Go* is called 'I'll Take Whatever.' The *Order, Pull Up, Check, and Go* is called 'Verification.' The *Order, Pull Up, and Wait* is called 'Special Orders Take Time.'

**Order, Pull Up, Grab, and Go**

Have you ever been deceived? Not that God is a Man that He should lie and not give us what we ask or desired, but there is another force at work here in the earth and that is the enemy. The enemy's job is to intercept anything that God is doing in our life. If we pull up and just grab whatever is handed to us, we do not know what we have. We are so focused on everything else that we miss out on what was intended for us and take whatever is given to us. Have you ever gone to the drive-thru and received the wrong order by mistake and you got home, work or so far from the restaurant before you realized that the order was not yours? How mad were you? You called back to complain and because you got attitude the person you are talking to gets smart and they say, "You should have checked the bag before you left." Do you try to eat what is in the bag when that is not what you had a taste for?

If the whole order is wrong, do you go back and lose all that time and gas? Then, if you do go back you wait for your original order to be completed and guess what, you are back in line waiting. The process did not change and being fast did not get you anywhere.

In life, shortcuts and being fast only have the outcome of going back and doing it all over again. We have to go back through the drive-thru and explain our situation then pull up. Because our order was special we have to *Pull Up and Wait*. They bring the order out and we look in the bag to make sure that our order is correct; it is. That inconvenience taught us a valuable lesson to always check our bag. Out of all that, they did not give you anything extra. It seems like as a common courtesy they would have thrown in a pie, cookie, an extra sandwich or something. But no, we got what we paid for.

The wonderful thing about God is that He will give us double for our trouble because He knows the length of our wait, the sacrifice, our patience, the desire of our heart, and the faith that it took for us to stay in line to receive the order. *Order, Pull Up, Grab, and Go* seems quick but it can be costly. We paid the price for what we are waiting on God to do by overcoming the tests and trials that we endured in life. If we disregard what we have overcome, that is like throwing something priceless away. How do we add up the cost for experience? Let's not take our eyes off our goals!

**Order, Pull Up, Check, and Go**

If we have prayed, planned, or saved for something that we have wanted a long time and we waited for it, that has become our expectation. We didn't get other things because we wanted this *specific* thing. We planned for it and it took time for us to wait it out. We are excited, and we place our order. When we get to the window and the cashier gives us the bag we do the Verification Check. This is when we verify to make sure that we receive what we asked for and we wait to see if everything is to our satisfaction before moving from the window. When we order something specific, we want to make sure that it is in the bag. Restaurants have peak times when they are really busy. When it is busy like that, things can go wrong fast, so we know that we have to be very attentive to our order. The same thing can happen in life, there can be so many things happening at one time that we can lose focus of the details of what we want.

If we have prayed, planned, and saved this took time and we don't want our efforts to be in vain. It is not that the whole order may be wrong, but a very important detail may be wrong that causes the meal to be bad. If we ordered a sandwich with extra cheese and no mayo and they gave us extra mayo and no cheese that changes the sandwich. If we were supposed to get the contract for $5,000 and they want to charge us $15,000, that changes the deal. We need to check the bag to make sure that we are getting what we ask for.

Have you ever been in a place where so much has happened, and you want to keep the faith and keep it moving, but you question what is going on? Verifying is checking with God to make sure that this is the right move to make. "Lord the last time I believed and had the faith for this and I thought it was going to work, it did not work." The only person that has all the answers is God. Who better to check with to see if you are doing the right thing?

# THE JEWEL OF POWER

When I was little, my aunt would take us with her when she went uptown and most of the time we went to McDonald's. I knew what was going to happen when we got there. She would order the food, get to the window to pay, get the bag and go through the whole bag and make sure everything was there. She would take her time, pull out everything in the bag one by one and then count the fries. If a sandwich was ordered special, she would unwrap it and check it to make sure that the sandwich was right and wrap the sandwich back up the same way they wrapped it when they gave it to her. Then she would put everything back in the bag. The same way they packed the bag that is the same way she repacked it. All while she is checking the bag we are looking through the rearview window at the people in the cars behind us throwing up their hands and making all kinds of gestures. I could read their lips saying, "What did she order?"

There were times when the order was wrong, and we sat there until they got it right. She would hold up the line and she did not care how many cars were behind her. That is the way we have to be about our promise. When it is our turn, it is our turn. We will not move until You bless us Lord! No matter what people say that are behind us. Let's not allow people to rush us along because they don't understand our process. It will do them good just to make it where they got to go.

When I was younger, I use to admire my great-grandparents. I watched them and I always dreamed of being married with a whole bunch of kids. They had 16, that was too many for me, but I wanted a lot of kids. Often, as I got older I would make the statement, "I want to be married." The first thing that would come out of some of my aunt's mouth were, "You better stay single as long as you can," or "Be careful what you ask for."

# THE JEWEL OF POWER

I get it. I know that there was a time in my life where I wasn't ready. Children imitate what they see and trust their parents who trust God. I wanted to imitate my grandparents and they trusted God. Faith is not about knowing everything or knowing everything to do, it is about being able to say, whatever happens, "He's got me."

I didn't know God, but I was around the things of God and I saw the things that He produced. The impression that I got was something was wrong with marriage, but I still had a strong desire for it. What concerned me was that no one asked me what I thought about marriage or what I knew about it? At least if there was a concern, they could have made sure that I didn't have a false picture about marriage or saw where my understanding was.

When the mature have experienced things, we have to make sure that we do not kill the purity of the dream of someone. This could apply to a business, school, or relocation. Sometimes our choice at the window can leave us a little sour. We have to make sure that we resolve any feelings that we have about our selection at the window.

Marriage is a great thing. For those with any influence, you have to make sure that you empower people so that they can make marriage work and last. Marriage is what people make it, if people don't work at it then it will not work. We can just look at people that have been together for years. They have had their ups and downs, but they work at their marriage because they are happy. Negative statements can make people think bad things about marriage and it can also reflect what their situation is.

We are human. No matter what our status is there are challenges and we are not going to escape them. Being single takes work too. Something is going to have a demand on our life whether it's God, church folk, children, job, family or all of those things combined. Everything has an advantage and a disadvantage. We will always learn something new about people we know because they are changing. Just like people will say, "There are no more good men or women in the world," or "All of them are either married or dead." I would say that also, until I realized that it was not true. There are good men and women in the world who are single, and they are looking and waiting to be found.

**Order, Pull Up, and Wait**

When we have a unique request that is special in every way, others may find it a little extreme. This desire that we have has been for something that we have wanted in a very specific way. Even though we could have had the order earlier, we do not want it that way, we want it the way we requested it. We place our order and pull up to pay when the cashier tells us that our *special order* will take some time because they have to cook it; there are none pre-made. We ought to be glad about that because they could give us something and call it what we ordered. It would then be an imitation of what we wanted. The cashier tells us that we will have to pull up and wait and someone will bring our order out to us when it is ready. We pull up and wait.

I don't know what your order is, but you will have to determine what the value of it is. Can you wait for it through the disappointments or through people telling you their opinion on how you should do it and the reasons why it is not working for you? You have to understand everybody's wait is not the same and some people just won't understand. Praise God they got theirs.

We will need line checkers to pray with us even if they may not understand the passion that we have for our wait, but they believe that God will be God and that His will be done in our lives. This is called the Power Moment. This decision can make or break a situation and it can determine the timeframe in which we receive our *special order*.

Just take a moment to think about what you are asking God for, waiting for, or expecting. It is important to you, right? If we are in line and we get to the window, we have a choice to make when the cashier says, "Sorry your order is not ready." We can pull up and wait or we can tell the cashier, "No thank you," request a refund, and leave.

If we have paid the price through our tests, trials, and persecution and God promised us something, we should not forfeit because we don't want to wait. That was the cost of the promise. Would you go in a furniture store and pick out what you want, pay for it, and then leave it because they took too long putting it on the truck? If you paid for something it is yours.

When we ask God for something and it does not happen right then, He is saying, "Yes, but wait." Do you tell God never mind? If we do that we will never receive anything because waiting is a part of the process. When it comes to what we have been waiting for, are we going to leave the promise and settle for less because we don't want to wait, and it isn't that important to us anymore? Can someone come along and persuade us to change our mind because what we are waiting for makes no sense to them? If we would only trust God enough to know that He can do it, we will have the courage to *Pull Up and Wait*.

Do you not know that you will be counted faithful because you believed? Genesis 22:1-14 says, *"Abraham was counted faithful."* God told Abraham to take his only son to sacrifice him. Abraham left the servants. He knew if he took the servants with them to build the altar he would have to do too much talking about the sacrifice and what God told him to do. He told them to stay there and await his return. Abraham had an expectation, do you?

Some things can't be explained because they will not make sense to people. If they do not have the right ear to hear, we are wasting our time, and this can frustrate our wait by trying to explain it. The main thing is if we are convinced of our promise, there is no need to try to explain it to others. Isaac asked his father where was the sacrifice and Abraham said that God would provide. Abraham had confidence that they both would come back. We have to have faith that, against all odds, that God will grant our petition.

For my single ladies, if we are waiting for our husband, wait with grace and class. Let's not be desperate, date a guy for meal, or let him in our Jewelry Box because we have no standards. When we are women with class and standards, some people say that we are too picky, superficial, think too much of ourselves, are high maintenance or have outrageous requests.

Having realistic standards is being wise. If we leave our Jewelry Box open, then all our valuables will be destroyed! If we want a husband who loves God, doesn't cheat, works, is not selfish or abusive, and loves his family, we need to wait on God for him. Those are some good qualities and they are not normal qualities for this world.

When we are single and take a stand to be single and say NO SEX before marriage that is setting us apart. If he cannot respect that, we can't waste our time with him. Sex is easy, the issue comes in when it is time to commit, converse, and build; can he do that?

# THE JEWEL OF POWER

As single women there are things that we should be doing to make ourselves presentable for our future husbands. We have to make sure that we are taking care of our health, finances, appearance, and planning for the future. I know that they always say that men are visual, and they think of sex 99.9% of the day, don't sleep on the sisters. Hello! Women we have to prepare to be that wife that he is expecting to have. God is faithful and as women we can't look at our age and get discouraged. However, don't leave what we have put good work into because we are disappointed in the timing.

We are women waiting to receive the promise of God and we have to continue on our journey. When we come into the knowledge of the Jewels that we possess, we learn not to just settle for the norm. We can't allow our worth to be appraised at a value lower than market value. We are the *Special Orders Take Time* women. We all tried that *Order, Pull Up, Grab, and Go* and got a mess. When we finally got rid of that mess, we did not even want anyone to mention their name, because we were not ordering that any more.

Your order may not be someone else's order and what you like they may not like. We have to respect everyone's process and wait.

**Jewel of Power**

The Jewel of Power is your authority to decide over your thoughts, situations, circumstances and to do the things that need to be done. When you have the power, your power needs to be controlled. You have to understand the value of the Jewel of Power because it contributes to your attitude and behavior, this will impact your promise. The way you operate in your power can be enough to power you through the wait; if you use it unwisely you may find yourself always settling because too much power can be dangerous in the wrong hands.

## *Declaration:*

God has a purpose for my life and I decree today that I will use the Power that is in me to live my life the way God intended. I reclaim all the areas of my life where I relinquished my Power to the enemy and to others. I realize that I cannot change my past or experiences, but with the Power that I have, I can change my future. I will use my Power to rebuild my confidence and I will share my life story to empower others who are on the journey of life.

# CHAPTER 12

*The Jewel of Possibilities*

*Opal*

Opal will inspire originality, boost creativity it has dynamic energy, intensity, enhances competency and efficiency.

Possibilities: a chance that something might exist happen or be true; the state or fact of being possible; something that might be done or might happen; something that is possible; abilities or qualities that could make someone or something better in the future.

# THE JEWEL OF POSSIBILITIES

In 1988 there was a movie called *Working Girl*, starring Melanie Griffith, Harrison Ford, and Sigourney Weaver. When a secretary's idea is stolen by her boss, she seizes an opportunity to steal it back by pretending she has her boss's job. Melanie Griffith played the secretary, Tess McGill, who aspires to be an executive. Tess worked at one job and was tricked into a date where she insulted an important colleague. She resigned from that job and that led her to work for Sigourney Weaver, who played Kathrine Parker.

Kathrine helps Tess to share her ideas. Tess suggests that a company, Trask Industries, invest in a radio station to gain position in the media. Kathrine tells Tess that she will pass the information along, but later tells Tess that it did not amount to anything. Later Kathrine breaks her leg and is unable to make it home and needs Tess to house sit.

Tess finds some papers where Kathrine is planning to use her ideas as her own. Tess sets up a meeting with Jack Trainer, who is played by Harrison Ford. Tess uses Kathrine's name to set up the meeting. Tess wants to meet Jack the evening before a party. They meet and end up sleeping with each other. However, Jack is Kathrine's man.

After Kathrine's leg heals she comes home the day of the meeting with Trask Industries. Tess leaves her appointment book and Kathrine learns of the meeting. The meeting is a success until Kathrine comes in and informs everyone that Tess is no more than a secretary and a fraud. Tess disagrees and leaves the meeting.

Tess comes back to the office a couple of days later to clean out her desk and she sees Kathrine, Jack, and Trask in the lobby elevator. Tess confronts Kathrine and tells her side of the story. Kathrine tries to distract the group, but Jack

# THE JEWEL OF POSSIBILITIES

says that he believes Tess. While Tess is talking, Trask hears something that gets his attention and he gets off the elevator. Trask gets in the elevator with Tess and Jack. Tess begins to tell Trask how she came up with the idea of the merger. When they all meet on the office floor, Trask asks Kathrine how she came up with the idea of the merger. Kathrine could not explain it. Kathrine was fired on the spot by Trask and Tess was hired.

    I love this story because it taught me throughout my life that no matter who steals my ideas, to not sweat it. I have been in positions where I have shared my ideas out loud. Others would take my ideas and claim them as their own. I always excelled at all the positions I held. I am a quick learner and I thrive on challenges.

    At first, I would be livid wanting to give them a piece of my mind and calling them out, but I did not say anything. I would go off by myself and cry. It hurt my feelings that people would smile in my face, ask questions and take my words as their own. I cried, not because I was weak, but because I was mad.

    I had to get my emotions right so that I did not snatch somebody up. I would talk to God and tell Him how unfair it was. I later learned it is called *growing pains*.

As I went through life, I found that this would happen more often than not and I wondered why. I began to learn that I was a leader and not a follower. This is not to say that I do not know how to follow, because a leader has to do both.

When I saw this movie, I looked at it over and over and I learned some valuable lessons. Do it before you get it; don't stop being just because someone wrongs you. People have ideas and sometimes they lack the confidence to speak up or they do not know how to formulate their words. But in any case, always recognize the person behind the idea.

I refer to what people say a lot. If I hear someone say something and I use it, I will say, "So and so said that or this," because the credit belongs to them. There is revelation behind everything and a reason why and how something came about. We do not have to have the high position to have a good idea, but we do want to follow the protocol when it comes to making suggestions about a new idea or a modification.

There are people that may have the position and salary but lack the confidence to do their jobs and they may become distracted by a person who has more confidence but is in a lower position because one day the person in the lower position may have the opportunity to shine. In whatever position we hold right now, whether we clean restrooms or are a doctor, we should do it to the best of our ability. The possibilities are endless, and we do not know where our hard work will lead.

Proverb 18:16 says, *"A man's gift will make room for him, and bring him before great men."* We don't know who is watching our work. If someone gives us a task to do, whether it is out of spite or not, use that opportunity to take pride in doing something well. The best way to get to this point in our lives is to have encounters with people in our life like the ones that do spiteful things toward us. I turned those things to my advantage and I made sure I still did my best; everyone around the situation is not spiteful. People are watching, and we never know who is watching to see how we will react to a bad situation.

Unfortunately, we are living in a time where we cannot wear our emotions on our sleeve. We must be able to take some things and not buckle at every hard thing; it is a war zone. We need warriors on our team and we need our teammates to know some moves too.

I am determined to walk in my own uniqueness, my gifts. So, steal my ideas if you want, claim them as your own if you want, but the TRUTH of it will always haunt you. The worst thing we can do is steal someone's ideas and walk in an identity that is not ours. If my name is Caprice, I cannot be walking around asking people to call me Michelle. Who will be me if I am trying to be someone else? When we step into that realm, we are saying, "God, You did not know what You were doing when You made me, so let me fix it."

If we do not know our identity, we cannot be left with the matters of the whole world, the beginning and end, so we just have to stick with the portion that was allotted to us by The One who knows it all. My name is at stake; your name is at stake. That means a lot and we should not allow things to steal our Possibilities of who God made and intended us to be. Those people with an identity crisis are the ones who cause the most chaos. They jump from trying to be like this person or that person without realizing that they are who they need to be.

Nobody comes in this world with everything figured out; this is some work. There are trials and errors, joys and pains. So, do not think we can come hijack the identity of someone without a cost. There are costs to be the person we are and if we steal another person's identity; that is FRAUD! There are various penalties to be paid for that.

We do not want to knowingly be in a position of identity theft because that leaves our Jewels exposed. Especially if we are trying to handle someone else's Jewels that we are not qualified to handle. Identity theft will leave us thinking we have the authentic Jewel and we have replicas, because they are stolen and imitated. The value of someone else's Jewels will not carry the same value for us. We will find ourselves fumbling over our words trying to come up with an answer that is a lie because we fail to recognize that our Jewels are for conquering something else. We will have to learn to walk in our Jewel of Possibilities. Just as no human is alike, our fingerprints are not the same, nor are our Possibilities. They are unique and designed just for us.

We cannot get something for nothing, so do the work and become the 'HER' we want to be. If we walk in other people's identity, we will have to keep changing things about that our identity. We may have to lie or be misleading because no one is the same. If we are confused every time we see something better about someone, we will change and that will change the valuable Jewels God has instilled in us that is for us to get to our purpose.

We each have gifts and we need to be confident in them. For those who don't know, I wanted the gift to sing. Lord knows that is what I wanted to do. Just know down in my soul, my voice is banging. My cousins can sing. I grew up with my cousin Hannah and she would sing like an angel. I would go off by myself and try to sing and I would be like, "NO!" I fought against not being able to sing for a long time until I was listening to a message and I got delivered. I learned from the message that I need to master my own gift. I learned that I do not have to be the one that can do something because if I know someone who can do it, that can be just as powerful.

Back to *Working Girl,* as women, we should be powerful, intelligent, confident, and hold our position in whatever role that we have. If someone takes our idea, it can only go but so far. When God has given something to us, He gave it to us so that we can develop it, and all will see how great our God is. When our mind begins to comprehend the Possibilities of what we have we will begin to see with supernatural eyes.

Let's be clear, God will not make us do something. There is always someone willing to do what God is asking, so don't be slow on the mission. God is so good at His creation. He could give everyone on earth an idea and each will be different, but how many would actually use the idea, or how many would look at someone else's idea and want their idea instead of the one that God has given to them? This is why we have to be so in tuned with US that we can hear, understand, commit and follow through with what is appointed to us in our walk and in our Possibilities.

We cannot be intimidated by anyone. Seize the moments to be around intelligent people, and this is where our confidence will show us where we are. Yes, it can make us nervous, but if life has brought us in the company of people who have become great, or are becoming great, we can't miss our opportunity. Embrace the moment and take mental notes.

I have been around people and while they were talking my mouth would be open in awe of what they were saying. I would be at the point of drooling. People with knowledge say things that they may consider insignificant, but when we do not know that information, it has a value that is priceless.

When we hear a person speak knowledge, it connects with something within us that hungers after it. We will treasure that which is precious to us and make sure that we hold it close to our collection of Jewels. When we know that, we can recognize that we are women that want more than we have and that all we need is an opportunity. There are POSSIBILITIES for you!

Don't be closed off to Possibilities because of what happened in the past. Shutting ourselves off to the promises of Possibilities will limit the extent of who we can be and who we can reach. Our goal is to allow the Jewel of Possibilities to be revealed.

I speak to your strength to grab hold of your Possibilities right now in Jesus' name. That you will come out and do what God has given you to do. I pray that the giver of Jewels will reveal your Possibilities and restore your opportunities so that you can live an extraordinary life.

My possibilities led to here, from a young girl with an extraordinary grandmother who loved God and showed me the way. I did not understand why my grandmother spent so much time talking and praying to God, but by and by I began to realize her purpose for it. I got saved in January of 2003 and on a Friday night, June 13, 2003, I received the gift of the Holy Ghost. I wanted to go to the graveyard dig my grandmother up, look her in the face and to tell her, "I Understand Now! I Get It!"

I knew she would not be able to hear me, but I just wanted her to know. When my path was not always clear or easy and I did not understand why the attacks were so vicious, I had the Jewel of Possibilities. Although my experiences may not be the prettiest, I have some Jewels that are priceless. I am a living witness that God is real. God changed my life, He used my low places to strengthen me to be able to walk tall and stand in the gap for those who have not developed and matured in their Jewels.

# THE JEWEL OF POSSIBILITIES

**Jewel of Possibilities**

It is the Jewel of Possibilities that will keep us going through life. Possibilities have a way of giving us a second wind to move again; to rise higher and to dare to be different. We do not have to do things like we have always done. Our Possibilities are undetermined. God will give us a voice that speaks out from the lowest places that we experienced to allow us to sit in a place of authority to call those out of darkness into His marvelous light.

*Declaration:*

My identity is tied in with my Possibilities and I believe it is possible for me to do the impossible. I believe in myself to create with the masterpiece that is within me. I will trust the connections that You give me to bring everything full circle. I will not worry about anyone stealing my identity, my creativity, or my vision because they are the keys to my future and this is what You have given me. I will walk in the authority of my Possibilities.

# ABOUT THE AUTHOR

Caprice, with a humble boldness, is the embodiment of her name. She is lioness on a mission to change the life of every woman that crosses her path. Just as her name suggests, she is the queen of the modern jungle we all inhabit.

This stunning, exquisite woman has endured many trials and difficulties in her life. After taking time to absorb the shock of the punches thrown to her by life, she has recovered, healed and is ready to do damage to the enemy's territory by training women everywhere to succeed in life through her powerful coaching and mentoring services.

Her motivational and instructional series 12 Jewels is a 3-program course that contains 4 modules each. She offers these series via webinars, live events, and as a sought-after national public speaker. She is committed to being the loudest cheerleader for all the women that seek her assistance in rebuilding and reshaping their lives. She has dedicated her life to helping women obtain possibilities that they were previously unaware even existed. Caprice has learned that change is unavoidable but is driven to help as many women as possible deal with life's unexpected challenges and difficulties change more effectively so that any struggles can be navigated by strategic and manageable solutions.

When Caprice is not fulfilling her mission to help women conquer over tragedies, defeats, broken relationships and addicts, she enjoys spending time with her family and friends in North Carolina and volunteering at her local church.

# CHOSEN JEWEL

## Connect with
## CAPRICE L. LYONS

A jewel, regardless of its origin and unique characteristics, has value. Just as each jewel in the world is different, so is each person. As women, each attribute that makes us different, makes us who we are and we should take pride in ourselves and our unique facial features, tone of voice, height, skin tone, hair texture, size, age, etc. We can be critical of ourselves and may even have a wish list of things that we would change if we could.

*Available at*

amazon.com       BARNES&NOBLE.com
                 www.bn.com

*Follow Me* @capricelyons   f  🐦  📷  in

*For more info, visit* www.capricelyons.com

www.ingramcontent.com/pod-product-compliance
Lightning Source LLC
Chambersburg PA
CBHW050202130526
44591CB00034B/1953